BEYOND THE WALLS

A CONGREGATIONAL GUIDE FOR LIFESTYLE RELATIONAL EVANGELISM

JAMES W. HOLLIS JR.

DISCIPLESHIP RESOURCES
MATERIALS FOR GROWTH IN CHRISTIAN FAITH AND LIFE

P.O. Box 189 • Nashville, TN 37202 • Phone (615) 340-7284

ISBN 0-88177-124-4

Library of Congress Catalog Card No. 93-71177

Unless otherwise indicated, all scripture quotations are taken from the New Revised Standard Version of the Holy Bible, © 1989 by the Division of Christian Education of the National Council of Churches of Christ in the United States of America and are used by permission.

DR124

❖ Contents

❖ Acknowledgments

I would like to thank so many brothers and sisters in Christ who have encouraged me in developing this book and the ministry upon which it is based.

First and most of all, I want to express my deepest love and appreciation to my wife, Jan, and my two sons, James and Jonathan, for having the Christian patience and love to bear with me through the years of ministering, leading, traveling, planning, and then writing. I could not have done it without you, my beautiful family from Christ.

I also wish to thank the thousands of laypersons who continue to inspire my life and ministry with their powerful witnesses in evangelistic ministry. I think of so many holy encounters that we have shared and of seeing your faces light up with the keen awareness that "the Holy Spirit is really using *me* to touch another life."

I appreciate all the local churches I have served as pastor. A special word of thanks and love goes out to the wonderful people of County Line United Methodist Church in Acworth, Georgia, for some of the most special years of ministry that I could have ever dreamed of sharing with any congregation. You will always have a special place in my heart and prayers. We shared the abundant life together, from Georgia to California.

I also owe a major debt of love to the faculty of Candler School of Theology of Emory University and to Dr. George Morris, Professor of Evangelism. You loved me and patiently shaped me for ministry. Growing up with numerous rumors about Candler being harmful to one's faith, I came to see that these rumors were far from the truth. Thanks for encouraging me to carry on, even in the midst of the valleys. I appreciate how the Lord has used you to broaden my horizons. Keep up your profound ministry.

My thanks would not be complete without expressing my great affection for the Emmaus Community. You have been a constant source of encouragement and love for me since my first Emmaus Walk. I have been honored and privileged to serve with you in shaping many new leaders for the local church. *De Colores* in the power of the Holy Spirit!

A final word of thanks goes to Stan England, National President of United Methodist Men and to Jim Snead, Associate General Secretary with The General Board of Discipleship for their affirmation. From the beginning, the Lord has used United Methodist Men in a special way to perpetuate this vision for the local church. May the Lord of all life continue to use all of us to meet needs, build relationships, and reach people with his love.

Jim Hollis
Proactive Evangelism Ministries, Inc.
6800 Green Oak Drive
Douglasville, GA
May 1993

❖ Preface

Come along on a great spiritual adventure. Discover the joy of Lifestyle Relational Evangelism. LRE is an adventure of listening to the Spirit's call for your life and responding to that call by risking yourself for the cause of Christ. It is a divine adventure of reclaiming the vast frontier of the unchurched for Jesus Christ. If you hear the call and come along, you will grow closer to Christ than you have ever been before.

Lifestyle Relational Evangelism is a specific kind of evangelism. It is a "lifestyle" because it is an exciting *way of life*; it is more than a program to be involved in at church one or two nights a week. Evangelism of this type happens wherever you are — in your home, in your neighborhood, at work, at school, and anywhere else in your community where you live, play, and become involved in the lives of others. "Lifestyle" in this sense has nothing to do with cultural style or personal taste; it has everything to do with *living* each day in touch with the Spirit and with the needs of others.

Evangelism is "relational" when it cares deeply about *human relationships* just as Jesus did. Sometimes evangelists have given a bad name to the good news of Jesus Christ by ignoring relationships — simply barging in where they were neither invited nor known, depositing their message, and leaving without further ado. How many of us have had the experience of trying to interrupt someone long enough to say that we are already seeking to grow in faith as Christians? By contrast, evangelism that is relational allows a genuine relationship to grow. It gets to know who people actually are. It looks for ways to be authentically helpful. And it waits patiently and hopefully for the right time to explore the mystery and the wonder of what God is doing in our lives and in our world.

All of this comes together in a particular way in the title phrase of this volume. The phrase "beyond the walls" refers not only to the walls of church buildings, but also to the walls of houses, places of work, schools, and other institutions within which we live our lives and have our being. Too many congregations today live their lives in splendid isolation behind the walls of church buildings as though their health did not depend on the quality of their life, service, and witness beyond the walls, in the surrounding community. Likewise, many people today live their lives in lonely isolation behind the walls of residences or places of work, no longer believing that a vital relationship with a faithful congregation is even possible. Lifestyle Relational Evangelism is a call to move out beyond the walls, to reconnect with the Spirit of God, and to rediscover the joy and adventure of life and faith in Christ.

Moving out in evangelism in this way can be compared with the early Methodist Circuit Riders who once rode the wilderness, daring to stand in the gap between isolated, needy people and the gospel. Beware, this territory can be dangerous; but God has promised to go with us. Some of your greatest future friends in life are there now, unaware of what Christ will mean in their lives and families. Some members of your congregation are there also, fully convinced that no one knows that they exist or that they need a new touch of the Master's hand. Becoming involved in LRE is stepping out in faith to be led by the Spirit to those who dwell on the frontier, behind closed doors — lost, isolated, needy.

Those who accept this invitation will embark on a great spiritual adventure. They will risk persecution and rejection. They will dare to love and give of themselves in the valleys of the vast frontier. Christ will go before them and use them in magnificent ways, beyond their greatest imaginings. They will refuse to limit their faith to the cloisters of church buildings. As a result, their congregations will experience profound spiritual growth. Motivated by the Spirit's call, they will go out to needy people in a lonely world for the sake of the One who died for all.

Now may God, who is able to keep you from falling and present you unstained before the glorious throne, be with you as you set out on this adventure of faith. It is my prayer that you will find the joy of Christ not only on the mountaintops but also in the valleys of the frontier. Let us do ministry more than we talk about it. Press on beyond the walls!

Part One

❖ 1. Beginnings

The summer of 1984 was pregnant with the sweetness of dreams and the bitterness of disappointment. The dreams belonged to the laity of a small, white-framed, country church named County Line. These dreams arose from prayers for a revival in their declining congregation. The disappointment belonged to me, a pastor who had planned for the United Methodist appointment system to send his family to a prominent church in Augusta instead of a place few had ever heard of named County Line. But isn't it amazing what can happen when the Lord has his way?

The Lord sent a revival to County Line and a thorough attitude adjustment to me in the summer of 1984. Because of his presence in this situation, strange and wonderful things began to take place. God's message to me was unmistakable, "Pound the pavement and knock on the doors — be faithful to me. Your people will go with you. Do it more than you talk about it."

First came Kevin Osoinach, the new youth minister, who arrived asking what we would do that summer. I asked him if he had good shoes. He asked where his office was to be located. I told him the same place as mine, in the streets and the homes of the community.

Next came Dale Dean, the chairperson of evangelism, and then there were three of us. Dale went to Jim Gaines, chairman of the administrative board, and asked him about his shoes. He said he could not go because he was cutting grass. For the next three hours Jim circled and clipped his lawn, wishing he had gone with Dale. The next time he did go. Then there were four.

Training on how to do house-to-house visitation began in the fall of 1984. A few more laity responded. Then there were ten. LRE was born and was growing. By now, what had begun as a vision had become reality. The Lord had raised a new work. By Christmas of 1984 County Line had become a household word in northeast Paulding and northwest Cobb County. Over 500 visits had been made at that point, and lives were changing in unbelievable ways.

Unchurched families began to come to church and enter new personal relationships with Jesus Christ. Some of County Line's own worst pessimists of the past were now going out every Thursday to knock on doors and share the wonderful news of revival. A new year came and so did the voices of a few skeptics.

"Well, Hollis, when the honeymoon is over, then you'll see how many of those lay-persons will continue all that visitation," predicted a voice of doom at a pastors' meeting in 1985.

Not all my colleagues were so skeptical. Some of them asked me to come to their congregations and share this new ministry with them. When I first told the laity of the invitation, it was hard for them to believe, but they were ready. In an old school bus we went to Tunnel Hill United Methodist Church in the Dalton District, thirty-seven strong going to another congregation to share a story of what the Lord was doing in an impossible situation. It seemed like a dream. We were living our dream.

Most of the laity group had never spoken in front of a congregation. It made little difference; Christ was in charge. They did a wonderful job and made many powerful witnesses at Tunnel Hill and at the next twenty-four congregations who invited us.

Who were these people? Fanatics? Radicals? Uninvolved folks in the local church? Heavens, no! They were all ages; one was nine years old and still another was seventy-seven years young. They were United Methodist Men, trustees, Sunday school teachers, administrative council officers, members of the finance committee, lay leaders, and delegates to the annual conference. Others were in United Methodist Youth, and many sang in the choir on Sunday. They were mainline United Methodists who were experiencing a revival in their local church. These committed Christians shared a simple story of what Christ could mean in the life of any local church. They were some of the finest ministers I had ever known. I began to wonder, "O Lord, what will happen next?"

In early 1986 the United Methodist Men of North Georgia endorsed this ministry as an official resource for spiritual growth. Several United Methodist Men's leaders in North Georgia had heard stirrings of a revival that was gaining strength through LRE. I was contacted by Stan England, the Conference President of United Methodist Men, and several leaders about a new relationship between United Methodist Men and LRE. The program committee for the North Georgia United Methodist Men invited a team from County Line to Rock Eagle Retreat Center for two weekends to teach sessions on Lifestyle Relational Evangelism. United Methodist Men were most encouraging and supportive of this ministry in its infancy. They supported it with fervent prayer. They carried it home with enthusiasm. They called me on the phone to tell me to keep on working on LRE, that someday it would be a ministry for all Methodism. I sensed in my heart a true kinship with United Methodist Men. They truly wanted revival in the church. They envisioned it coming to pass. I was not sure what this would mean. It still all seemed unreal to me, even as more and more laity got involved in the ministry and as the level of love in our church soared.

In the summer of 1986 I found myself going on vacation to San Francisco with my family and with my wife's parents. We planned to visit their relatives whom they had not seen in fourteen years. The experience was similar to that of the appointment system: being sent somewhere you would prefer not to go and having to be optimistic about all the potential you were assured was waiting there. We arrived on a Tuesday. The relatives were not sure what it would mean to have a Methodist minister in their home since they were unchurched at that time. On Thursday they popped the big question, "Are you planning to attend church on Sunday?"

I told them that we would like to, but refused to participate in the selection of where to go. By the weekend they had searched the Yellow Pages and newspapers trying to find just the right congregation. We quietly entered St. John United Methodist Church that Sunday, a totally unfamiliar congregation, unknown to everyone in our families. As we listened, the time of prayers came. The pastor began to share names and other needs to be remembered.

He said, "Let us continue to pray for our new efforts to begin a visitation ministry. We have searched for help and have found none. However, let us continue to pray faithfully that the Lord will send someone to help us with this at St. John." You could have knocked me over with a feather.

Before I knew what was happening, my father-in-law rose to his feet and said, "Praise the Lord, your prayers about some help for visitation have been answered." After the service we shared with them the story of Lifestyle Relational Evangelism and they invited me to teach a session on LRE one evening while I was there.

I held a seminar, and a good group of St. John's laity went out to knock on doors for the first time. Their pastor, Dave Bunjie, showed tremendous enthusiasm and gave strong encouragement to his people. They invited me to come back in the fall. I told them that when I returned I wanted it to be with the laity of County Line. They felt that if the Lord got me there once, surely he could bring us all back. It would be impossible without Christ.

Things began to happen in California. The pastor of St. John talked to his superintendent; the superintendent contacted leaders at the Conference level. The excitement spread. We received an invitation from the California-Nevada Conference to come to San Francisco, January 21-25, 1987, to introduce their people to Lifestyle Relational Evangelism. The invitation also included the laity from County Line. Bob Bridges, our district superintendent, said he would like to make the trip with us. His unwavering support has been a continual encouragement in the development of this ministry.

As I watched twenty-one of us board the Delta L-10-11 in Atlanta for San Francisco, I fondly thought of our old school bus which had carried us on earlier trips. I never knew it would be like this. One of the laity who went on this trip, Mrs. Waunette Cantrell, was a young seventy-eight and had never been near a jet. People forget their limitations when the Holy Spirit is leading.

When we got to San Francisco International Airport, the people from St. John, Los Altos, and several other congregations were there to greet us. No one could have shown us warmer hospitality than these California United Methodists. They took us into their homes and into their hearts, and we truly had all things in common. We sang hymns of the faith together. We worshiped together. We laughed together. We shared dreams and fears. We went out in teams into the San Francisco area to knock on doors for Christ and for The United Methodist Church. Nearly every door had a "No Solicitation" sign posted, but I reminded the laity of the congregations that we were not soliciting, we were giving love away. We saw many doors open and tears in the eyes of lonely people. Some said they had never had a stranger come to their home before that day. They invited us in and we saw new relationships begin. While in California visiting, we were blessed to meet with Bishop Leontine Kelly, in her office in downtown San Francisco. She extended greetings to us on behalf of her conference and had prayer for us and for our ministry efforts. I will never forget the grace and love she shared with those of us from a little church called County Line.

St. John became the flagship congregation for LRE in its conference. Many new families came into the congregation because of this ministry. We made new friends we will never forget. We saw victories some thought would be impossible. My wife's relatives not only became members of St. John but leaders in that congregation over the next few years. The laity of County Line and I were invited to go back into the California-Nevada Conference for a second trip that was beyond our greatest expectations.

Then we received invitations to go into the Kentucky Conference from First United Methodist Church in Somerset. What joyous days we shared with the people of the area around the mighty Cumberland River as we went out with them to knock on doors. We had shared this ministry in yet another area of the country. We made more ministry trips to Somerset as the congregation worked to expand this ministry. The pastor, the staff, and the laity of that congregation were committed to the ministry of evangelism. I will never forget two physicians, Dr. Kelly and Dr. Betts, who inspired the laity of that congregation.

In the fall of 1986 we returned to Rock Eagle Retreat Center to lead workshops in Lifestyle Relational Evangelism for two weekends. The folks at County Line and I were deeply moved, participating and hearing laity from churches we had shared with earlier (such as St. Luke's, Bethel, and Level Creek) share what Lifestyle Relational Evangelism had meant to their congregations. A spirit of revival was going on in those places through this ministry.

Another new and unforeseen opportunity for ministry opened up when a team from County Line was invited on an evangelism mission to Monterey, Mexico. We shared Lifestyle Relational Evangelism there. It was a wonderful time in which the Lord touched many lives. What a blessing it was for all of us to share with Randy and Jean Healan, a missionary couple from the North Georgia Conference, and to have the opportunity to see the tremendous love the Lord has given them for the mission field.

The Christians in Mexico gave us far more than we could give to them. Their hearts overflowed with love. The trip was powerful and we saw many persons in the Monterey area come to Jesus Christ during our services and teaching sessions. On the morning we left, Randy gave me an envelope with some scripture passages he said the Lord had given him concerning our ministry. One from Isaiah 43:18-19 reads:

> *Do not remember the former things, or consider the things of old.*
> *I am about to do a new thing; now it springs forth, do you not perceive it?*
> *I will make a way in the wilderness and rivers in the desert.*

So what happened at County Line? On Thursday nights alone, over 3,500 visits were completed into community homes by the laity of the congregation. On Sunday nights *Evangelism Explosion* became part of our congregation, which functioned in tandem with LRE. Tuesday mornings we began to visit those unable to attend church and a number of older adults. In 1987 we began a program of "Membership Care" for members of the church. Over forty laity became involved in these ministries. The County Line budget increased by over 120 percent and average attendance increased by over 60 percent. With only *two* walk-in families in two and one-half years, the church added over seventy-five new members. The membership approached 300.

Though numbers are exciting, they are *not* what Lifestyle Relational Evangelism is about. Too many United Methodist congregations today are statistically strong but spiritually dying. As John Wesley said of many persons in the Church of England in his day, "They have the form of religion without the power." Wesley viewed this as a certain note of doom for the church. It is my conviction that most United Methodists today long for a meaningful, solid revival to take place in the life of their local church.

Our local churches don't need more experts to tell us how much trouble we are facing. We don't need more analysis of how we got this way. We do need to do something about it and we need to do it *now*. Lifestyle Relational Evangelism is a ministry that was born in a particular congregation of The United Methodist Church. It provides an effective way to cause an ongoing, consistent, and solid spiritual revival in other United Methodist congregations across the United States.

LRE can happen in your local church. It is happening in local churches today. Pioneers in this ministry are still sharing their experiences across the denomination. Our desire is to share with congregations, not as "experts" but as servants in ministry. It is our goal to see local churches become centers of practical evangelism in their respective communities. To this end, I (the author) have recently been appointed as an approved Conference Evangelist with the North Georgia Conference of The United Methodist Church in order to devote full time to this ministry across North America. For further information, see Introduction to Training Sessions on pages 81-83.

We need your prayers even now. Would you please lift us to the Lord and ask that he continue to raise the spirit of evangelism across the Christian faith?

Defining Lifestyle Relational Evangelism

Lifestyle Relational Evangelism is a ministry that seeks to relate to persons at the point of their greatest needs through the establishment of meaningful, caring relationships. We tie this to the life and total ministry of the local church.

The ministry has two major aims. One is to lead persons into a personal relationship with Jesus Christ. The second is to lead others into a meaningful life of discipleship and servanthood in a local church. This ministry does not, however, always use a direct approach in seeking to accomplish these two major aims. LRE recognizes that for many people the direct approach is not the wisest way to seek to establish meaningful and lasting relationships.

Lifestyle Relational Evangelism's major emphasis is not concerned primarily with numbers and statistics. Numbers can be arranged in a variety of ways by creative minds, and statistics can be manipulated to prove almost anything. LRE's major emphasis is ministering to the needs of others and establishing ongoing relationships. Tremendously strong statistics can appear to represent great evangelism, when they are actually the result of something else entirely.

Consider, for example, a church located in an area of booming population growth. In a sample calendar year this church has over 750 persons who walk into the sanctuary on their own. In that same year, 250 of those folks decide they like the congregation and choose to become members. Of the 250 who join, 100 of them were already United Methodists who desired transfer, 75 were members of other denominations, and another 45 of these were already preparatory members of the church who came in through a confirmation class. The remaining 30 new members were spouses and children of the first 100 who had never joined a church previously. Is this evangelism? Or is it something else?

What is the rest of the story? The rest of the story may be that over 30,000 new families moved within a five-mile radius of this local church in the same year those 250 joined. This church may not have an ongoing program of outreach of any kind to unchurched families in their community. They simply visit the visitors and express satisfaction. When the pastor is asked about an outreach ministry, he or she states that one cannot even keep up with the visitors, much less visit those who are unchurched!

This church may have activities that will keep the 250 new members involved, but did they join the congregation through outreach evangelism? This is hardly true. What about the other 500 walk-ins who did not join? Where did they go?

Lifestyle Relational Evangelism is not a ministry that goes into the neighborhood or community in order to see how many *decisions* can be made for Christ. When Jesus instructed the disciples to go into the world, he told them to make disciples, not just to get decisions. Decisions can come quickly, often before persons making decisions really understand the statements they are asked to repeat. Seeing a person make a new decision for Christ can bring great joy, but decisions are only a small part of the process of discipleship.

Discipleship comes from spending time with people on the long, joyful, and sometimes tedious road of relationship. When we walk this road with others, outside the church, we must consistently live the Christian life. We will demonstrate the gospel as we live before them. Discipleship was what Jesus was about in the New Testament. The preponderance of evidence in the Bible teaches us that God does want the church to grow through evangelism centered on building relationships, resulting in lasting discipleship and service.

Hundreds of programs are offered today that seek to accomplish a variety of goals. Some are intent upon playing the game of multiplication of the church rolls to have the greatest bragging rights. Others are out to get people to make *decisions* for Christ. Still others are in the business of making money in the name of religion and at the expense of anyone who will listen. It must be said that *any program not based on a genuine concern for the needs of others is not worthy of the name of Christ.*

Lifestyle Relational Evangelism patiently demonstrates caring for the needs of others. These needs may be physical or spiritual. When involved with this approach, one learns to show love to others regardless of their response to that love. Evangelizing in this way should make neither the visitors nor those receiving a visit uncomfortable.

Everyone has needs. Discovering and meeting the needs of others is not done through quick and easy programs. The discovery of needs comes through diligent service and careful listening. Pride or arrogance may lead us to try to tell others what their real needs are, rather than being content to listen to them as they tell their story. Our sin is that we feel *our* story is the most important one. This sin, fully conceived, brings forth the fruit of self-righteousness. Little else on the face of the earth is as ugly to behold as a pietistic, self-righteous, judgmental Christian. Such Christians exist as a most effective weapon in the arsenal of evil. From this we can see that one's *motivation* is crucial to the establishment of a ministry of evangelism.

At the same time it must be said that evangelism is going out to reach the lost and the unchurched, with the emphasis on *going*. Jesus said, "*Go* into all the world, and make disciples." He did not wait around for disciples to come to him. Evangelism has a definite element of risk. To go out we must be committed and willing to risk ourselves in ministry for the building of God's kingdom.

Can you picture what this kind of evangelism would mean for the mainstream church? Speaking only for The United Methodist Church, we would no longer be a group of fine folk who wait for visitors to show up in a worship service; no, we would be mainstream Christianity in the community, carrying the church into the homes of people who know themselves to be lost, isolated, and needy. We would no longer resign this vast field to charlatans and cults who parade about in the name of Christ. Untold numbers of unchurched people would experience the warmth and love of United Methodism in their living rooms and dens, in their front yards, and on their porches. Children of unchurched families would begin to ask their parents, "Can we go to worship and be with those caring people on Sunday morning?" This would be a long overdue beginning of the recovery of the great frontier of the unchurched.

Who Leads LRE?

Someone is needed in every congregation to light the fires of a genuine ministry of outreach evangelism, if that ministry is to burn brightly. Most congregations have a committee known as the committee on evangelism or the outreach committee who might be looked to for leadership. In far too many local churches, however, this committee is somewhat inactive, if it exists at all. All too often, the primary task of such committees is to handle revivals and special worship events at some time during the year. Such special events are important, but they are not the same thing as ongoing outreach evangelism.

Likewise, the pastor or staff could carry the fire of evangelistic ministry, but that is often viewed as expected behavior for preachers and staffs. Evangelistic power is often dampened by apathy if the spark comes from the staff alone. In many cases, moreover, it is much more effective for one layperson to invite another layperson to become involved in evangelistic ministry than for a pastor to make the invitation. In every congregation, however, there are many lay people who are waiting eagerly and patiently for the opportunity to be involved in genuine outreach evangelism.

One of the principles of Lifestyle Relational Evangelism is *comradeship in ministry* for the laity of the church. This proves crucially important to the effectiveness of this ministry. It leads to ownership of ministry rather than making lay people feel like "helpers" of some-one else's ministry. Too many positions in local churches discourage creativity of the laity. They become viewed as jobs of necessity instead of opportunities for creativity and joy. Their functions are sometimes limited by the church staff's thinking or by the pastor's inter-pretation of how they should be carried out. Laity should not feel as if they are under the critical scrutiny of the pastor or the church staff as they participate in ministry. This is one sure way to choke the ownership of ministry and cripple the morale of the local church.

Comradeship in ministry does *not* mean that a pastor should never invite people to get involved in the ministry. Nevertheless, a personal invitation from the pastor is usually more effective than general appeals from the pulpit or in the church newsletter. Pastors must show sensitivity or laity will perceive that they are being invited once again to only "assist the pastor," rather than to discover their own unique ministry with the Risen Christ.

Wesley and the early Methodists knew the importance of laity in evangelism at the grassroots level. Where the early Methodist lay people worked, they witnessed and shared the gospel. In the places they went for socials, they told others of what took place in the com-munity of faith and how it changed their lives. We must come to that place again today in the local churches across this continent and around the world. Every situation is an opportunity to witness to the power and presence of the Living Christ by sharing his love and grace.

Let me illustrate this from personal experience. One night as we assembled for visitation, I asked to go with a layman of our congregation, Jim Gaines, into his ministry area. Entering the subdivision of nearly 200 homes, Jim Gaines turned to me and said, "You know, Jim, these are my parishioners and in many ways I feel like a pastor to them, reaching out to them each week with the love of Christ."

The thought overwhelmed me as a member of the ordained clergy. Then it occurred to me and I said to him, "You *are* their pastor, Jim! You are the only witness from the church some of them have ever known. I'm proud to be with you and to see the effectiveness of your ministry to these people. I am sure they see Jesus in you."

A Special Role for Men

This introduction of LRE would not be complete if we did not place special emphasis on the great potential for *men* to become key leaders and supporters. Please understand. This is not a call for the exclusion of anyone. Groups and individuals of any description — male and female, old and young, lay and clergy — can sponsor LRE, and are encouraged to do so. Among all of the individuals and groups in a congregation who are ready and able to support a ministry such as this, however, one group should not be overlooked — men. In many congregations, men are accepted as the true movers and shakers, yet the men's group is often like a sleeping giant.

There is no limit to what can happen spiritually in a local church when the men of the congregation as a group receive spiritual motivation for evangelistic ministry. We have already mentioned how the United Methodist Men in Georgia played a key role in helping to launch and inspire LRE in their state. The same thing could happen in other states (or with other men's groups in other denominations) as well. The national and conference organizations of United Methodist Men are already known for providing enormous motivation and support for missions across the globe. Picture a similar concentration of effort in the ministry of local church evangelism; the potential for good is soul-stirring.

United Methodist Men truly desire to see something profound take place spiritually in The United Methodist Church. What can they do? They can help coordinate and participate in LRE. They can go out consistently into the field of need in the community surrounding their congregations. They can play a major role in motivating and encouraging the laity of the congregation to live a *lifestyle of relational evangelism*. They can also play a special role in encouraging laity and clergy to work side by side as fellow ministers in the local church. In two words, they can *sponsor* and *model* LRE in their congregation. As this occurs, we will see a dramatic change in the direction of our denomination. We will see thousands who hunger for friendship and care, respond to the old, old story of the Christian faith. As the men of the church — the husbands, fathers, and brothers of countless others — take the lead in reaching out for Christ, others will be pulled into a groundswell of ministry, a groundswell that could reach across the denomination.

Special instructions are included in Appendix A for organizing your local chapter of United Methodist Men to launch, guide, and support LRE. These instructions show how your United Methodist Men leaders can lead in developing a total ministry of Lifestyle Relational Evangelism in your congregation or conference. (Other groups and individuals in The United Methodist Church or in other denominations may also find some of these instructions helpful.)

I believe the Holy Spirit is stirring United Methodist Men to be a vital part of the next great awakening of Christianity in the world. The endorsement of LRE as an official program of the United Methodist Men unit of the General Board of Discipleship shows that national United Methodist Men leaders share this vision. Now, together, we wait eagerly to see what will happen when United Methodist Men in congregations across the country take hold of this vision for ministry into the next century. They are clearly willing to risk themselves for Christ! Risk in ministry makes the difference. It is a high and holy calling. The more we risk ourselves in ministry for the kingdom, the closer we get to one another and to the King of kings. Press on. Move out beyond the walls with Christ.

❖ 2. Biblical Foundations

The ministry of Lifestyle Relational Evangelism is firmly grounded in the Bible. According to the New Testament, Jesus went out to people across the geographical areas of his time to meet others at the point of their greatest needs. He did not sit in a church office in downtown Jerusalem waiting for people to come to him. He sought them out, taking the initiative for ministry.

Jesus also taught the disciples by the method of "modeling." He not only told them what to do in ministry, he daily *showed* them how to be ministry in the world. Jesus lived as the world's greatest example of a caring person in action. He constantly went into the fields of need, healing and inspiring others. Then as he prepared to leave his earthly existence, he gave very specific instructions to his disciples. Consider the following:

> *Now the eleven disciples went to Galilee, to the mountain to which Jesus had directed them. When they saw him, they worshiped him; but some doubted. And Jesus came and said to them, "All authority in heaven and on earth has been given to me. Go therefore and make disciples of all nations, baptizing them in the name of the Father and of the Son and of the Holy Spirit, and teaching them to obey everything that I have commanded you.And remember, I am with you always, to the end of the age (Matthew 28:16-20).*

As we mentioned in the first chapter, one of the greatest misunderstandings Christians have about evangelism is that our focus should be on getting people to make decisions for Christ. As we reflect on the above text, commonly referred to as the Great Commission, several things become quite obvious.

We are not called to get decisions but to *make disciples* for Christ. There is an enormous difference between these two concepts. If we focus on getting decisions, then that will be our primary goal as we go to visit with others. That cannot be our primary goal, however, because our calling is to *demonstrate the gospel*, not simply to make an *intellectual presentation* of it. How can we illustrate this in ministry?

Let's suppose a visitation team from the church is going to call on a prospective family. After a few moments of casual conversation about the weather, the dog, and the local news, the team turns the conversation to a spiritual focus. They begin by sharing a brief testimony about the local church, in which they share how wonderful and loving the local church is to them and how it could be for this new prospective family. Next the team members move the conversation onto a more personal level, sharing some of their own testimonies concerning how they came to decide to receive Jesus Christ in their lives. From there the focus shifts to the prospective family. Now all spotlights shine on the prospects.

Using several of various possible questions, the new family is asked if they are aware of how they can become Christians. Then they are asked (nearly always point blank) if they have made a personal decision for Jesus Christ. The tension level soars in the room. It is so thick you could nearly slice it with a knife. But the manual for this kind of approach says we should not worry about that. It is expected as part of this procedure. So the team presses on relentlessly in pursuing an appropriate answer which matches their list of correct responses.

If the prospective family does not respond correctly (in the judgment of the team), then the family is given an intellectual presentation of the gospel and invited to respond immediately with a decision concerning this presentation.

Suppose all goes well in the questions and in the presentation. Then the moment of all moments comes and the team asks the family member or members, "Is this the decision that you would like to make now?" The family members say, "Yes." A time follows in which prayer is shared for the family making a profession of faith and then a time of celebration. Is all well now? Not necessarily.

I have personally been on calls like this. Certainly there have been times when persons have made decisions and have been quite sincere; a divine appointment occurred. These persons came into the local church and became disciples, living out their faith. In most cases, however, this is not what happens. In most cases, people either make a hasty decision in the pressure of the moment — a decision that they are not really ready to keep in good faith — or they react to the strange visitors who have forced them so abruptly to discuss something so important and so intimate as their spiritual journey. When an intellectual presentation of the gospel turns in the latter direction, even though everyone tries to remain courteous and open, all feel a strain of relationship. Even so, some Christians find it quite unexplainable why such visits can become heavy in tone and spirit.

The reason is not that hard to understand. When we try to move the level of relationship from that of a brand new acquaintance to that of intense discussion on personal spiritual issues — without any real process of getting to know one another in between — we quite simply experience a great crash. We have taken someone's hand and heart, with little or no basis of relationship, and we have asked them to move miles on their faith journey in only a small number of minutes! Such a leap of faith certainly *can* happen; but, let's be honest, most of the time it will not and, as a result, we will leave a messy trail of relational debris from the crashes we have created.

Families who have experienced such visits often feel abused, used, and manipulated by the team making the presentation. If they should say "No" to the momentous questions about accepting Jesus, then they have walked into a lose-lose situation that they did not design. We lose the opportunity of entering into a real and caring relationship that could lead to the genuine discussion of spiritual questions; they lose the opportunity to consider their decision about Christ in the light of such a relationship. Was their decision a good one? No, not in the light of who Christ is and what he brings to the healing of human life. Did the decision reflect an informed understanding of Christ and, therefore, a deliberate rejection of him? Probably not; in any event, we may never know, for how can we continue this kind of relationship? We will be in the recovery mode at best. Why not listen again to the words of our Lord as he talks about evangelism?

Jesus says, "Go therefore and *make disciples*," never using the word *decision* even one time in the text. Of course, making a personal decision for Christ is part of discipleship! But discipleship is a process which occurs most effectively on a solid foundation of relationship. Then there is not the pressure to decide right now, but in a person's heart time — whether in five minutes or five months. In the meantime, the prospective family is loved, ministered to, and cared for with the love of Jesus Christ. Persons are given space and time to move toward their decision in a gentle way through the patient demonstration of the grace of our Lord. People will not always respond the way we anticipate, regardless of our approach; but our calling to relate to them in caring ways does not change for all of that.

So, if we follow the biblical example of Jesus, we will make discipleship, not decisions, our number one priority. But how do we really do that? According to Jesus, we focus on discipleship by being sensitive and responsive to the needs of others. Consider the following scripture:

> *When they had finished breakfast, Jesus said to Simon Peter, "Simon son of John, do you love me more than these?" He said to him, "Yes, Lord; you know that I love you." Jesus said to him, "Feed my lambs." A second time he said to him, "Simon son of John, do you love me?" He said to him, "Yes, Lord; you know that I love you." Jesus said to him, "Tend my sheep." He said to him the third time, "Simon son of John, do you love me?" Peter felt hurt because he said to him the third time, "Do you love me?" And he said to him, "Lord, you know everything; you know that I love you." Jesus said to him, "Feed my sheep" (John 21:15-17).*

The point of this memorable dialogue between Jesus and Peter is clear: As Jesus' disciples we are to feed his sheep (the people) and meet their needs; indeed, that is how we actually demonstrate our love for Jesus Christ. In order to really live this out, however, we will have to be ready to meet others without imposing a predetermined agenda. We will have to be the kind of people who are secure enough in our own faith to allow the substance of our visits with others to flow from their immediate needs, interests, and questions.

Let me give an example. Many families today are facing the crushing reality of unemployment. For a family to lose its major source of income is a devastating prospect — financially, emotionally, psychologically, and spiritually. This places constant stress on the family; they need someone to care enough to listen to these needs and to respond to them in a loving, caring way. We can listen and we can do everything within our power to link them with resources that will help them through this stressful time in their lives. Perhaps our congregation can even assist them financially or offer some hope for them in the way of a job prospect. At the very least, we can lift them in prayer and let them know we hear their pain and stress.

Entering into a family crisis with caring and compassion in this way is a phenomenal witness to the meaning and purpose of the local church. It is immensely more powerful and meaningful than brochures or advertisements in the Yellow Pages. In such moments of sharing, the family being visited actually comes to experience — in their greatest moment of need, right where they live — the richness of what the church is about. In a very real way, they experience "church." This is incarnational evangelism at its finest. We will never experience these things if we stay inside the walls of our local church buildings. We must go on the great adventure of visitation ministry.

Thus, along with the emphases on discipleship and meeting needs, the biblical mandate for LRE also includes the experience of *being sent*. Since the days of Jesus, being sent forth has proved to be one of the most profound of spiritual experiences. Consider the following passage:

After this the Lord appointed seventy others and sent them on ahead of him in pairs to every town and place where he himself intended to go. He said to them, "The harvest is plentiful, but the laborers are few; therefore ask the Lord of the harvest to send out laborers into his harvest. Go your way. See, I am sending you out like lambs into the midst of wolves. . . . Whoever listens to you listens to me, and whoever rejects you rejects me, and whoever rejects me rejects the one who sent me." The seventy returned with joy, saying, "Lord, in your name even the demons submit to us!" He said to them, "I watched Satan fall from heaven like a flash of lightning. See, I have given you authority to tread on snakes and scorpions, and over all the power of the enemy; and nothing will hurt you. Nevertheless, do not rejoice at this, that the spirits submit to you, but rejoice that your names are written in heaven." . . . Then turning to the disciples, Jesus said to them privately, "Blessed are the eyes that see what you see! For I tell you that many prophets and kings desired to see what you see, but did not see it, and to hear what you hear, but did not hear it" (Luke 10:1-3, 16-20, 23).

Evangelism in the biblical mode involves being sent. All that we have said thus far about building relationships and meeting needs is consistent with this. Jesus sent the disciples out into the field of need — to meet people where they lived, to build relationships, to make disciples — but let's be candid, being sent can be scary. Some Christians today may find this the most difficult part of LRE. Must we go out to meet others and to make ourselves vulnerable to strangers? Can't we wait for people with needs to come and find us? Jesus' model is clear. He sent the disciples forth into the field of need.

Jesus did not ignore questions of risk and danger when he sent the first disciples. He warned them that they would feel outnumbered, even overwhelmed — "the harvest is plentiful, but the laborers are few." Still he sent them and urged them to pray for courage and for coworkers. Likewise, he warned the first disciples that they would experience danger, risk, and vulnerability — "I send you out as lambs in the midst of wolves." Still he sent them, and he gave them instructions about how to keep their fears and hopes in perspective.

Jesus' words to the first disciples are also his words to us. When we go out into the field of need, we will at times experience rejection; but we go not as representatives of ourselves, nor even of our congregation in itself, but as representatives of the Lord of Life — " He who hears you hears me, and he who rejects you rejects me. . . ." Indeed, it is the Lord of the Harvest who is ultimately rejected or accepted. Likewise, Jesus puts our successes in perspective. As we go out, some people will be open to us; they will receive our help; they will welcome us into personal relationship. Indeed, we may see remarkable spiritual renewal or healing; "even the demons" may be subject. The most important thing, however, is that we know the joy of a relationship with the living God — our names "are written in heaven."

The ultimate joy of being sent, then, centers in this relationship with God and in the awesome experience of being used of God to extend this relationship to others: "Prophets and kings desired to see what you see. . . ." If we do not go, we will never know what Jesus meant. What could be more powerful spiritually than the great adventure of reaching out, having been sent like the original seventy? Little else comes close to providing us with this kind of spiritual growth. We are called to experience the joy of the great frontier, to celebrate the assurance of our eternal relationship with Christ, and to extend the joy of this relationship to others.

Now someone may want to say to me at this point: "Jim, this is all fine; LRE is clearly a gentle and caring approach to evangelism. It places the highest value on building relationships and meeting needs; but, for all of that, it seems to be naive about the spiritual forces at stake in such an enterprise. The scripture passages you have given so far do not mention the pivotal events of the gospel — the cross of Christ, his resurrection, and our response in faith. Can evangelism really take place without confronting spiritual resistance to the proclamation of these events?"

These are important questions. I understand their point, but an immediate rejoinder must be given: The emphasis in LRE on building relationships and meeting needs, far from being naive about the dangers of spiritual resistance to the gospel, is fully aware of these dangers and proceeds as it does precisely in order to preserve and celebrate the power of the gospel. In order to address these matters more fully, let us consider one additional passage from the Book of Revelation:

> *Now war arose in heaven, Michael and his angels fighting against the dragon; and the dragon and his angels fought, but they were defeated and there was no longer any place for them in heaven. And the great dragon was thrown down, that ancient serpent, who is called the Devil and Satan, the deceiver of the whole world he was thrown down to the earth, and his angels were thrown down with him. And I heard a loud voice in heaven, saying, "Now the salvation and the power and the kingdom of our God and the authority of his Christ have come, for the accuser of our brethren has been thrown down, who accuses them day and night before our God. And they have conquered him by the blood of the Lamb and by the word of their testimony, for they loved not their lives even unto death. Rejoice then, you heavens and those who dwell in them! But woe to the earth and the sea, for the devil has come down to you with great wrath, because he knows that his time is short!" (Revelation 12:7-12).*

Here in one sweeping vision is a description of the awesome spiritual conflict in which the ministry of the church is engaged. According to the biblical vision, God is engaged in a terminal conflict with evil, and the church has a key role to play in this conflict. On one side stands Satan, the great accuser, whose lies and accusations have worked to separate people throughout history from the love of God and from each other. On the other side stand the people of God who overcome these lies and are reconciled to God and to one another by "the blood of the Lamb," by "the word of their testimony," and by the fact that they "loved not their lives even unto death." Here is a spiritual vision of the church in its most intense form, but how does this vision relate to the gentle practice of LRE?

The vision foresees, first of all, that the people of God overcome the accuser "by the blood of the Lamb." The central mystery of the Christian faith is the power of salvation made available to all through the blood of the Lamb of God. This is an event to which Christians return again and again in scripture and in worship in order to probe the mystery of faith and to grow in the way of discipleship. For those who have begun the journey of Christian faith, the cross of Christ and his resurrection is the clearest expression of God's unconquerable love, forgiveness, and friendship. It is the power of salvation. For those outside the faith, however, these events may seem strange and grotesque. Moreover, the language in which these events are described needs the context of Christian experience and community (relationship), or it may sound like nothing more than a scary, intellectual "formula" for salvation.

Here, then, is the first response to my imagined objectors. Building relationships and meeting needs is not a sideline of the gospel; it is the essence of the gospel. What does the blood of the Lamb do, if it does not meet needs and heal relationships between God and God's people? To build relationships and to meet needs, therefore, is already to live in the reconciling power of the gospel, and to confront the accusing forces of darkness. The task is by no means easy. It requires grace, patience, and faith beyond sight. Christians must ultimately speak of the cross, of the blood of the Lamb, and of many other things that reveal the mysteries of faith; but an unchurched person's desire to explore the meaning of these mysteries may not begin until he or she experiences firsthand what it is like to witness the love of Christ in relationship with others.

To use the language of faith in its most intense form on an actual visit with an unchurched individual or family would in many cases be both insensitive and potentially intimidating to those being visited. To be effective in using the principles of LRE, we must work hard to be relationally sensitive, to build bridges of communication, and to demonstrate the love of Christ in action. The world does not believe that the Christian community has meaningful answers for today's needs. As Christians we know that the gospel holds the answers. If, however, we botch our efforts to build bridges of caring relationship, then those being visited may never really hear the gospel because they will not feel loved enough to ask any questions. Therefore, we must temper our boldness with sensitivity in order to represent the cause of the risen living Christ.

Does this mean that Christians involved in LRE will never use the traditional language of faith to describe their experiences of God, church, and world? By no means. The second means of victory among the people of God according to the vision of John is "the word of their testimony." There is a poverty of testimony in the local church today. In days of old, on the American frontier, testimonies provided much of the freshness of Christian experience. Persons were given opportunity to tell others what Jesus Christ meant in their lives. This was a tremendous source of affirmation and encouragement for all who gathered with the community of faith — believers and seekers alike. But notice, the context for sharing such testimonies was not, in the first place, a visit with strangers; rather it was the gathering of the people of God for worship.

We can recover the spirit of vitality in the local church by involving laity more significantly in worship and in sharing faith. Worship is not a spectator sport with only a few players on the field and a crowd of onlookers in the grandstand. The very word *liturgy* means the work of the people of God. Testimonies shared by laity during worship and other meetings of the local church provide a rich source of inspiration and teaching for the entire covenant community. The enemy was conquered, the voice said, by the word of their testimony. As laity go out into the field of need in their community, and return to the community of faith for counsel and encouragement, there will be much to share about the infinite ways of the Spirit who leads them. While the specific accounts will all be quite different, the unifying theme will be strangely familiar — God is using me directly to touch another life for the kingdom that has no end.

Let me illustrate this from the practice of ministry. I vividly recall a ministry team coming to a reporting session one evening, where they told about meeting a couple who said they were new in the community. The team was invited in and had a nice visit. A few weeks later the team returned and again found the couple at home. The reception this time was equally warm but the team leader noticed a certain uneasiness in the air.

The next Sunday the couple came to church for the 11:00 service. They were quite friendly and outgoing. I recall meeting them on their way out of worship. Later that week I received a phone call from them.

"When the team from your congregation came to our house, we were not sure how to feel. We felt that God was reaching out to us. We were going to get up and come to church the very next week but only got ready and sat and stared at each other, thinking we couldn't go to church since we're not married. A couple of weeks later the team came back, more friendly than ever! We decided that the love we felt from them was more powerful than worrying about our circumstance and that we would go anyway — just to see if everyone else was that nice. While we were in worship that Sunday the Lord spoke to us and we felt the need to repent of our relationship, to give our lives fully to Christ, and to become a Christian couple. We are now married and would like to join your congregation as new Christians."

They did join the congregation, and became highly involved members. She went on to teach Sunday school. He became involved in LRE. Their ministries as Christians have continued to expand in ever new directions. They will never be the same because of a team who dared to go house to house in the field of need — a team committed to showing the love and forgiveness of Christ in relationships without having to force a full and immediate confrontation with the mystery of the gospel, a team representing a congregation where testimonies of grace and faith could be heard in worship and where laypersons could witness that grace at work in the lives of other laypersons. Today, the testimonies of that team and of that couple enrich the entire congregation and join with yet others to overcome the lies of the accuser by the blood of the Lamb. That, friends, is the gospel in action.

Here then is my second response to the imagined objector. There is a time to speak directly and boldly of the pivotal events of the mystery of faith, and a time to wait. The time to speak certainly includes those occasions when Christians gather to worship, study, and encourage one another in the community of faith. This does not mean that unchurched persons will never hear these conversations. Indeed, on the basis of growing relationships, there is every reason to invite unchurched friends to attend worship, and every reason to hope that many of them will overhear the gospel and want to explore more deeply what the faith of this community is about. As individual relationships grow, moreover, specific people will find themselves drawn to conversations about spiritual things. Unchurched persons will know that their Christian friends care deeply about them, and they will want to know why. As some of them learn the language of faith, and come to understand in their own experience the treasure of God's love in Christ, they will know that Christ himself cared enough to send someone to seek them out, even them. All of this, however, requires sensitivity to the timing of the Spirit and to the needs and joys of building relationships.

What then of the final means of victory mentioned in our passage: They "loved not their lives even unto death." In a way this sums up everything we have been saying. To become involved in outreach evangelism with LRE requires that we as Christians have a vision that is larger than our own lives, centered in Christ, and patiently to wait for his timing in our own lives and in the lives of others. We can wait and hope in this way because, to paraphrase the old hymn, "We know whom we have believed, and are persuaded that he is able to keep that which we've committed unto him against that day" (#714, *The United Methodist Hymnal*). As a result of this eternal perspective, we are willing to be fools for Christ, to lay down our lives in service and relationship with others. Temporary mood changes and even tough circumstances do not deter those who go in the power of the Risen Christ. They sense an ultimate purpose and desire to be used to the uttermost by him who called and said, "Go."

In this light, building relationships in the name of Christ, meeting needs for the sake of the kingdom, going out into the field of need, is not simply a gentle way of doing evangelism; it is a demanding and rigorous way of living in the power of the gospel. That is why we call it *lifestyle* relational evangelism. By contrast, to always insist on confronting people right away with the mysteries of faith is inconsistent with the spiritual and relational concern of the gospel. Where this has happened, it is no wonder that many unchurched people have turned away from the church before they ever really had a chance to understand the blood of the Lamb.

Isaiah sensed a new stirring of God's Spirit in his day. He rallied the people of God and called them forth to ministry. He spoke for God, challenging the people with a message that is still relevant for the church today:

> *"I am about to do a new thing; now it springs forth, do you not perceive it? I will make a way in the wilderness and rivers in the desert. The wild animals will honor me, the jackals and the ostriches; for I give water in the wilderness, rivers in the desert, to give drink to my chosen people, the people whom I formed for myself so that they might declare my praise" (Isaiah 43:19-21).*

Jesus Christ is calling us today to wake up and do a new (and yet an old) thing. He is calling the church to be intentional about going out into the field of need to reach persons who will never walk into a local church on their own initiative. In his book *How to Reach Secular People*, George Hunter speaks of the "ignostics" — people who have no reference point to the Christian faith. We live in a land populated by ignostics — millions of people who know little or nothing about the central events of the Christian faith, but who are waiting for new friends, desiring community, caring, and love. We can be the generation to go and love them into the kingdom. God wants to do a new thing through the church today; every Christian can have an exciting, life-transforming part of this new-old thing called reaching out in the love of Jesus Christ. The fields are white unto harvest. Pray the Lord of the harvest to send laborers into his harvest! Then go, and become an answer to prayer! Press on, beyond the walls with Christ.

❖ 3. Meeting Needs

The vast majority of persons in North America today are not closely connected or intimately involved in any local church. In nearly every community, large or small, rich or poor, urban or rural, "the fields are white unto harvest." We live in a land that needs missionaries. The church is called to reach out to these millions of families and individuals, but in order to reach out in meaningful ways, we need to understand who the people are.

The Unchurched

To begin with, we need to recognize that many people in our culture have *never* been meaningfully involved in a congregation. We are not speaking here of inactive church members, or of persons temporarily out of contact due to a move or an illness. We are speaking of that vast group of North Americans who for one reason or another have concluded that the church is quite simply not for them. How did they come to such a negative conclusion about the church? There are no doubt as many reasons as there are people. We should not underestimate, however, the power of the mass media in our culture.

All of us in North American culture are familiar with a certain negative stereotype of the church and organized religion. We have seen sitcoms that portray the church as interested in only one thing — money. We have seen movies that portray Christians, and preachers in particular, as inept and out of touch with reality. Needless to say, these media have had considerable help from news reports concerning television evangelists such as Jim Bakker and Jimmy Swaggart. As Christians we don't need to deny that these stereotypes exist. The problem, however, is that many unchurched persons have no meaningful Christian background against which to measure the stereotype. They are stuck with the mass media image: Christians are either bumbling idiots or fanatical zealots.

The negative stereotype of the church is further reinforced by the techniques and activities of various religious sects and cultic groups on the scene today. Countless homes have been invaded by the pressure and manipulation of such groups. Cults and sects often present themselves in Christian clothing only to assault people at a later time with insensitivity and coercion. As a result, many unchurched families almost automatically assume that anyone on their doorstep is there for some harmful religious reason.

This is the atmosphere into which we move as Christians from the mainstream. At one time the mainstream denominations carried tremendous respect, but many decades have passed since we ventured into the field of need with open hearts and hands. As a result, unchurched people know little about our identity or witness. When we find courage once again to go out, they will expect almost anything from us but that for which we are really there — to build open and caring relationships. It will take time, patience, and grace to overcome these stereotypes that have developed across the years.

There is good news. People are responsive to sincere caring. They long to see an end to loneliness and insensitivity. They are receptive to people of real faith who cut through the stereotype, but this places a major responsibility upon us. If we are to cut through the stereotype, we must approach others with our minds and hearts truly set on building caring relationships. Such caring, furthermore, is not simply a commercial for the church. Authentic caring is not conditioned on receiving a positive response about the church or even about one's own person as a representative of the church. We shall look in more detail at factors that strengthen or inhibit genuine caring. For now, we simply register that this is a major area of sensitivity to unchurched persons. Many of them have great needs. They, like us, live in what is often a lonely, hurting, and impersonal world. Christ can use us to bring healing and transformation to many.

Inactive Members

Inactive members compose another major group of people who are not currently involved in a congregation. As the name for this group implies, inactives are members who joined a congregation at some time in the past — perhaps they were even actively involved at one time. But they no longer are. Beyond this general notion, however, what defines an inactive member? Is it someone who only comes to church once a year? Is it someone who is a member of the "T.E.C.H. Club," persons who attend only on Thanksgiving, Easter, Christmas, and Homecoming? Perhaps it is the person who sends his or her offering but never shows up at any activity. For purposes of LRE, we shall define an inactive member as follows:

> An inactive member is an individual who has been baptized and has joined the church, but who is not presently active or committed to any organized ministry of the local church and is not regularly present at the principal weekly worship services.

This definition presupposes that all members of the local church are called to be actively involved in some form of ministry in the congregation to which they are related. It also implies that members of the local church need to be consistently involved in weekly worship with their congregation. Both of these assumptions are grounded, moreover, on the understanding that when persons join a congregation they are, in the deepest spiritual sense, becoming members of the Body of Christ. To use the traditional language of the church, they have repented and received forgiveness for sin and have entered into a personal relationship with Jesus Christ as their Savior and Lord. In reality, however, this is not always the case.

As a pastor of almost twenty years I am grievously aware that we have members on the rolls of our congregations who have never known what it means to experience a personal relationship with Jesus Christ. Far too many people have been received into membership as though they were joining a civic club or a secular organization, but that is a very different setting. To make matters worse, it is sometimes very difficult for people, once they have joined the membership roll of a congregation, to understand or to see the need for an experience of repentance, forgiveness, and faith in Christ. All of this has implications for ministry to inactive members.

Ministry to inactives requires that we learn to see with spiritual eyes — that is, to see not only their inactivity, but also their needs, their hopes, and their integrity. For far too many years we have been plagued by a false and misleading attitude concerning inactive members: "They know where the church is and they can come just as easily as we can. I just don't know why they are not coming anymore, but I have already invited them back."

In spiritual terms, this is an attitude of disastrous judgmentalism. What if God took the same attitude toward us when we fall away at different points in our lives? We might get what we deserve, but we would not receive what God's grace supplies. Grace is the key to understanding and ministering to inactive members of the local church.

Think with me for a moment about the scope of grace. Before we are ever born into this world, God is reaching out toward us with prevenient grace. As we are born and begin to grow, God's prevenient grace sustains our existence, enlivens our minds, and reaches out to us in a million different relationships, both personal and natural. *Prevenient grace* is the term we use in the Wesleyan tradition to refer to the power of God's goodness reaching out to us even before we ask for it or know what to call it. Every opportunity we have ever had to flourish and grow in life — indeed, the created world itself — all is interwoven with this grace. Such grace is full of wonder for us. It rains alike on the just and the unjust. Yet it is not unmindful of human sin or unmoved by human sorrow — and it is not cheap.

As Christians we know that we are bought with a price — the price of a cross. Jesus died for each of us — from the most upstanding person in the community to the lowest form of human degradation. In this way, the love given through prevenient grace in creation has been reconfirmed in the clearest way for all time. God's love is universal; it embraces all persons equally. Still, the magnitude of this grace is strangely easy to forget. As active Christians we can become easily frustrated with others when they seem unwilling to maintain their commitment to Christ and to the church. We may reach out to them once or twice (invite them back to worship), but then we find that our sense of grace is far more limited than God's; we let ourselves become frustrated, indifferent, or even judgmental toward our inactive friends.

Ministry to inactive members requires divine resources of persistent patience, unconditional love, and unshakable hope. Research has shown that approximately twenty contacts are required to restore a meaningful relationship with an inactive member. Only about fifteen contacts are required to reach an unchurched person in the same way. This shows that ministry to inactives calls for a double portion of patience, coupled with an attitude of persistence that is geared for the long haul. If we believe that inactive church members will be reached again just by inviting them back, we will certainly be disappointed.

Along with patience, ministry to inactives requires love — the kind of unconditional love described in the New Testament. The New Testament (Greek) word for this kind of love is *agape*. Such love, according to the apostle Paul, "keeps no record of wrongs" and "always perseveres" (1 Corinthians 13). Agape love is a gift of the Holy Spirit at work in our hearts. It enables us to look beyond the faults of others in order to see their needs. It strengthens us to build caring relationships based on genuine giving and receiving. It is entirely consistent with God's love and forgiveness in Christ. It is the way we came to Christ.

Agape love is a requirement, because inactive members often feel deep resistance to the idea of becoming active again. General church appeals through correspondence or campaigns will not reach them. There are reasons why they have fallen away. Some of the reasons may be negative or even hostile. Are we prepared to listen to the true feelings of inactives without becoming defensive, angry, or hurt? God calls us to reach out with agape love to inactive members with all of the compassion of the Holy Spirit, keeping in mind that Jesus gave his life for these very persons.

There is no way to overemphasize the importance of these considerations. As you organize teams for visitation (see Chapters 5 and 6), you will want to build this new ministry on a foundation of prayer. The first few times you meet together as a team, devote yourselves to prayer for the task before you. Ask the Holy Spirit to give caring and compassionate hearts to you as you begin this venture into the unknown. Pray for patience and agape love, fully aware that inactive membership is a deep-seated problem for which there is no quick fix.

Along with patience and agape love, the effort to reach inactives must be grounded in hope. This hope, however, is not about improving attendance or church budget figures; rather, it is about rebuilding real, honest, and caring relationships. There is nothing so sad as having to acknowledge that your congregation has visited its inactive members only once in the last year, and then to ask for money. By contrast, the hope of LRE is to build new relationships with inactives, to give them an opportunity to share their true feelings, and to make a tangible witness that the church really does care for them. Whether they become involved again is *not* the most important consideration. Our faithfulness in reaching out with agape love is the number one priority. We leave the results to the Holy Spirit, knowing that everything we do will be used to the glory of God.

At the same time, we should emphasize that visiting with inactives requires a positive, supportive attitude toward the local church on the part of the team. If the persons on the visitation team are not absolutely positive about the local church, how can they possibly win someone back? The team's positive regard for their congregation can be contagious; it may become a vehicle toward involvement for the inactive members as well. So often a kind word can turn away wrath. The more positive and affirming the team members can be about the local church and its leaders, the more effective their ministry will become.

Blending patience, love, and hope on a visit with inactives takes wisdom and discernment. Team members should encourage inactives to share their true feelings completely, but not in order to dwell on the past. Remember, the ministry team may be able to help the inactive members find some closure on their hurts, angers, or feelings of indifference toward the church. As those being visited share their pain, they may also experience some sense of relief or release from the things that have oppressed their relationship to the local church. Team members should be sensitive to such moments and affirm what is taking place. When possible, such release should be celebrated and put to rest as a part of history. Prayers can be offered on such occasions, to bring closure and a clear hope of moving on to something new and brighter.

Inactive members will not usually return to the church until they are able to see themselves as accepted and loved again by their church family. If this love and acceptance is not communicated by the visitation team, it may never be communicated at all. This entire process takes a tremendous investment of time and energy. It will not happen quickly or easily, but the return of an inactive individual or family to authentic relationship in the local church is cause for tremendous joy, learning, and celebration. Typically, once they return, the inactives will become fully involved in ministry.

Before we leave the topic of inactive members, let's look a bit more closely at why people become inactive in the first place, and what the local church can do to avoid this. Simply put, people become inactive because they were never really incorporated into the ministry and fellowship of the congregation. The first six months of a new member's life in the congregation is vitally important in determining his or her future level of involvement. During this time, the new member will evaluate how caring the church really is. If the new member is incorporated in major ways into the ministry of the congregation during these six months, he or she will probably be a highly active, contributing, and participating member in the future. If, on the other hand, the new member is not meaningfully engaged in some form of ministry in the first six months, then he or she can easily drift away into inactivity.

What can congregations do to avoid this? First, congregations must abandon the deadly notion that people are really involved just because they have joined the membership roll. This is an illusion in most cases. When people join the church they have merely approached the beginning of involvement. Many new persons have little working knowledge of the local church and its ministries. They do not understand how decisions are made and who is responsible for what. They can relate somewhat to the persons who helped them in their decision to join, but even this is only a beginning.

Second, congregations need to provide a sponsor to stay in touch with new members for at least six months. Otherwise, who will notice if they don't attend worship for three weeks in a row? Who will seek to involve them in a Sunday school class, a small group, or a ministry team? Who will continue to build a meaningful relationship with them after they say "I do" to all the questions of membership?

When inactive members come back into the local church, they need much the same kind of care as new members. Persons who have been inactive for long periods of time will discover that things are different since they quit coming. They may feel insecure or uncomfortable. Just like a new member, the inactive will often benefit from having a sponsor for the first six months. Has the inactive member become regular in worship attendance? Has he or she gotten involved in an area of ministry? Naturally such matters must be handled in strict confidence; the goal is to help inactive members, not to embarrass them.

In addition, inactive members may require some special care when they return. This is the case, for example, if the members became inactive due to conflict or offense. Those who were actively involved in rebuilding the relationship in the first place — the original visiting team — are good candidates for sponsor because they will probably know something of this background. If none of these can serve as sponsor, then it may be helpful for them to be involved in the selection and training of a sponsor. The sponsor does not need to know every detail of the conflicted background. No confidences should be compromised. Still, it may help the sponsor to know that the returning member has previously experienced pain or conflict in the congregation.

Ideally, there should be no inactive members in the local church. Surveys show, however, that many congregations are satisfied when their active attendance averages only 50 percent of their membership roll. This is a tragedy. To be an inactive member in such a congregation is a dangerous spiritual condition. Most local churches are not doing anything — either by accident or design — to minister to these persons who are a part of the kingdom of God. Let's make certain that our church is an exception to this widespread norm of the 1990s. Let's allow the Holy Spirit to use us to reach out to our inactives, realizing that they are one of our greatest undeveloped resources today. God calls us to win them again to the fold.

Moving Members

People move for many reasons — a lost job, a new job, a transfer, a family illness, or just a desire to live in another place. No matter why people move, however, the church can be far more intentional about caring for them when they do. Let's consider just one possible scenario.

A husband in his twenties has a good job working for a large national company. He likes his work. He has a lovely wife and a ten-month-old daughter at home. His wife also works part-time and they are quite involved in the local church. They attend church more than 70 percent of the time. He plays softball and works with Scouting. She sings in the choir and is in a United Methodist Women group. Life is grand.

Then, on a Tuesday afternoon, he walks into their home with a pained expression on his face. His wife notices immediately. He has to tell her that the company has ordered him to transfer from New Orleans (their home of four years) to Chicago. He can hardly speak about it. They both feel numb at this news. Every friend they have is in their local church. Every relative is close by. They hate cold weather. They are victims of a company shuffle.

They share their news with their Sunday school class. Their friends are also upset, but they try to be encouraging. They hug them and shed tears with them over the news. He will have to leave in three weeks. The couple put their house on the market, but there seem to be no prospective buyers. They decide she must stay behind to sell the house. Weeks go by and the house still does not sell. She slips toward becoming inactive because of depression and having formerly shared duties to do alone. She prays and misses her husband. She cries after their daughter goes to sleep.

Someone asks about the couple at church. The response is, "Oh, they've been transferred to Chicago." This is only partially true; the part that is false is tragically false. This couple is now one of the most critically hurting couples in the membership of the church, but who will be intentional about ministering to them so long as they can be described simply as "transferred to Chicago"?

Someone might respond, "Well, if that was our congregation, things would be different!" Nevertheless, people like this couple get lost all the time in the cracks between the busy activities of the church. They have involuntarily been exiled to the ranks of the inactive, but they need their congregation now more than ever. This does not have to happen.

Suppose that congregation had an intentional ministry of Lifestyle Relational Evangelism in place and one facet of the ministry was to care for moving members. This couple would have been cared for in a disciplined way. First, they would have been shown empathy and concern in an ongoing manner. The congregation described above was empathetic at first, but as the news of the move grew cold, the couple was finally counted simply as "having been transferred."

What is more, a congregation with an LRE ministry to moving members might have recognized this family in a special worship service of commissioning and sending forth — perhaps even before the husband had to leave. As a result, a much larger segment of the congregational family would have been aware of the situation and able to respond. The base of caring in the congregation would have been broadened. The gifts, talents, and ministry of the couple would have been recognized. The couple could have been sent to Chicago to begin their new adventure in life and ministry, all with the supporting prayers of their former congregation.

Finally, an LRE ministry to moving members could also have maintained supportive contact with the wife and child. The women of the church could have made a schedule to check on her needs. The staff could have scheduled her in the visitation ministry, and helped with child care arrangements. Others could have offered help or expertise in selling the home. Someone could have invited her and her daughter out for Sunday lunch. This would have allowed her to know and experience the continuing care of her congregation — in spite of the move.

The reason this does not happen enough in local churches is not because the people are not loving; they simply have not been intentional in designing ministries for this group of persons. Any local church that thinks this through can do an excellent job of caring for families who are moving. Let's allow our awareness to rise to a new level *now* so this never happens to anyone else in any congregation.

Special support for this area of ministry is available to United Methodists. Since 1981, the ministry of United Methodist Men has included resources and a telephone referral service for keeping track of United Methodists who are moving. When a member is moving, the pastor or other local church leader simply contacts the national hotline for moving Methodists located in the United Methodist Men offices in Nashville, Tennessee (1-800-624-4130; persons in Alaska, Hawaii, or Tennessee can call collect 615-340-7127). The United Methodist Men staff will register information about the move — name of moving member, name and address of current congregation, destination address for moving member, etc. — and convey this information to local church and denominational leaders in the new area. Imagine how supportive it is for a moving member to be received in a strange new city by a warm, caring group of United Methodist friends. This can happen every time someone moves if the local church will do its part.

Ministry Referrals

Ministry referrals are another group of persons who need the ministry of LRE. A ministry referral is someone who is involved in one of the activities of the local church but has no other meaningful, spiritual connection with the congregation. Examples of activities that often include ministry referrals are: Boy Scouts, Girl Scouts, softball teams, soccer teams, and other sports activities. Likewise, various community support ministries (Parents' Day Out) and self-help groups (diet groups, exercise groups, etc.) frequently include ministry referrals.

Since ministry referrals are involved in a group activity but are not intentionally involved in the spiritual life of the congregation, they present a special test case for the principles of relational evangelism. On the one hand, they come to the activity groups because of some felt *need* — support, instruction, friendship, exercise, fun. Further, they stay with the activity groups because they have found a *relationship* with others that in some way meets their needs. On the other hand, they may not see any connection between their activity in the group and the larger spiritual vision of the congregation. They are receiving ministry, but they might not call it that. Indeed, some participants might even resist the suggestion that a connection exists. How will an LRE congregation relate to these persons?

The key to this area of ministry is a close working relationship between the leaders of the congregation and the leaders of the various activity groups. Simply put, all of these leaders need to share a common understanding of the connection between the activity groups and the larger spiritual vision of the congregation. We affirmed this connection above when we described how the spiritual vision of God's reconciling love is already engaged through activities that build caring relationships and meet real needs. When the leaders of various groups understand this connection, they are in a position to affirm with the congregation the value of the activity groups in themselves, yet also to remain sensitive to the importance of ministry referral.

Leaders are called to practice discernment. Many persons who become involved in activity groups are, after all, seekers. Indeed, experience has shown that ministry referrals are among the most eager to hear the gospel and to explore the call to discipleship. And why should this not be so? They have already been involved with other members of the congregation in the kinds of relationships that reflect the love of God in Christ. Their experience of caring relationships in their groups will often touch their own deeper spiritual concerns.

At the same time, leaders must practice patience, love, and hope with those who, for whatever reason, are not ready to consider the call to discipleship. Not all participants in every activity group will want to move further into the spiritual life of the congregation, even when friendships with existing members of the congregation have been formed. If the leaders of the activity groups, like the members of the congregation, are genuine in their commitment to the principles of LRE, they can affirm the activity groups — the relationships formed and the needs met — as valuable in themselves. The participants do not have to recognize the spiritual vision or join the congregation for these other values to be affirmed. There is no place here for thinking of the activity groups as a pretense for a hidden spiritual agenda. Building relationships and meeting needs is the spiritual agenda.

What if the leader of an activity group cannot affirm the spiritual vision of LRE? Christians do not have to agree with others about the motivation or meaning of an activity in order to affirm its value. Nevertheless, when leaders are at odds, the effectiveness of ministry can be compromised at all levels. Activity leaders who oppose the congregation's spiritual vision should be affirmed, loved, and cared for, but they must also be replaced in leadership in order to preserve the integrity of the congregation's total ministry.

When the leaders of the activity groups work closely with a specific team of the LRE ministry, these kinds of dynamics can be handled with confidence and genuine care. The LRE team assigned to ministry referrals should meet weekly with the leaders of the activity groups to build relationships, explore needs, and discuss vision. The local church should evaluate its ministries from time to time to insure that every program offered is genuinely connected to the ultimate cause — to know and share the love of God made known in Jesus Christ.

Worship Visitors

More United Methodist congregations than ever before are getting serious about ministry to worship visitors. Worship visitors are persons who walk into a local church with no previous personal contact or invitation. Such visitors are one of the greatest gifts God gives any congregation. Worship visitors are seekers. They are often looking for new spiritual direction and relationship. However, they will not automatically continue to visit unless they find genuine signs of the relationships they are seeking.

Visitors need personal contact and affirmation from the local church. Research has shown that the first contact should occur during the first twenty-four to forty-eight hours. An LRE worship visitation team, for example, might make a personal call on the afternoon of the Sunday that the visitor first attends. This first contact is a natural time to be creative in showing hospitality. Take something more than words to leave with the visitor — homemade pies or cookies, or a plant. Some congregations have even created a special container for delivering goodies — a cup or plate with the name of the congregation or an engraving of the church building on it; or a specially decorated pot appropriate for home or office. The possibilities for hospitality are endless. Be creative and take your gift with a smile and love in your heart for those whose search has brought them into contact with your congregation.

Follow-up with worship visitors is essential. People who visit in your congregation may also be visiting elsewhere. That is often the nature of a search for spiritual roots and community. Your LRE ministry will want to keep careful attendance records for all visitors. Have some visitors returned each week for several Sundays? Perhaps their needs are being met in some way. Follow-up contacts may clarify how the congregation can best serve. Have other visitors indicated by spotty attendance that their search is more ambivalent? A follow-up visit may reveal special needs that call for attention, or that they are finding a stronger connection elsewhere.

In keeping with the whole spirit of LRE, follow-up contacts should not be pushy. Demonstrate respect for the needs and desires of visitors, including their desire to visit elsewhere. Call again after they have not attended for three weeks or so to see how they are doing and to let them know that you are still thinking of them. This type of gentle follow-up will show your respect for their needs and wishes, but it will also show your genuine care and concern. If worship visitors finally decide to become involved elsewhere, give them your warmest wishes, let them know it was nice to meet them, be glad that their search is leading in a specific direction and, if you have opportunity, ask them to pray for you.

In addition to a visitation program, your LRE ministry to worship visitors will also benefit from a coordinated ministry of greeters and ushers. Greeters and ushers are not the same thing. The primary responsibility of greeters is to meet visitors outside the building and to help them find their way into the building. The primary responsibility of ushers, by contrast, is to serve visitors once they have come into the sanctuary to worship. Let's look at each of these roles in turn.

Greeters are a special team of caring members who locate themselves outside the church building — near the front door, perhaps, or at the edge of the parking lot — in order to welcome visitors as they arrive. The longest walk a visitor may face on his or her first Sunday is from the car to the pew. Greeters are trained, therefore, to understand that the quality of caring for worship visitors begins as soon as they approach the church building. A helpful resource for this ministry is the booklet, *Ushering and Greeting*, available from Discipleship Resources.

Due to their position outside the building, greeters give visitors an immediate sense of the warmth of the congregation. To be sure, everyone in the congregation should be friendly and warm, but we all know that this is not always the case. We never get a second chance to make a first impression, so the impression the greeters make is of prime importance.

Sunday school classes, senior citizens' groups, United Methodist Men, United Methodist Women — each group could choose a certain Sunday or Sundays during the year to serve as greeters. To have a well organized ministry of greeters is to make this first impression with discipline and intentionality, rather than leaving such impressions to chance.

Along with welcoming visitors and learning their names, greeters have a special opportunity to serve. Is the visitor looking for a particular part of the building? Some visitors may need to locate the nursery or a Sunday school class for a specific age level. Since visitors themselves come in all age groups, greeters too should include girls, boys, women, and men. Greeters do not, however, simply point visitors toward a location in the building. Rather, greeters serve as personal hosts for the congregation. Each visitor is personally escorted to the appropriate area, whether that be the sanctuary, the nursery, or another location. If the visitors are arriving for worship, the greeters should walk with them into the narthex or vestibule of the sanctuary and introduce them to one of the ushers.

Just as greeters are responsible for what takes place outside the sanctuary, ushers are responsible for what takes place inside. For purposes of LRE, however, the ministry of ushering itself needs to be reconsidered. Indeed, some traditional notions of ushering can get in the way of the LRE emphasis on meeting needs and building relationships.

Consider, for example, some of your own experiences with ushers. Have you ever entered a sanctuary where the usher handed you a bulletin, smiled at you for two seconds, and then promptly resumed a distant gaze like a soldier on guard at Buckingham Palace? Some ushers seem to have been trained to stand perfectly still as though their feet are nailed to the floor. Their vocabularies are limited to short phrases such as "Hi," "Good Morning," or the lengthy, "Nice to see you." This school of ushering also dictates that ushers should frown during the offering, as though they are having a very bad day. Congregations that accept this kind of ushering do not need a Sunday afternoon visitation ministry; only the toughest of visitors, looking for an unfriendly place to sit alone for an hour, will come back. Such a congregation will not meet needs or build relationships.

By contrast, a vital ministry of ushering will express warmth, courtesy, and genuine care. Greeters will be sure that visitors are introduced to an usher, and ushers will do everything in their power to receive the visitors with grace and to help them find a warm and welcome place to sit with others during worship.

With a little forethought, the task of seating visitors can become a ministry in itself. Isn't it amazing how people love to sit in the same areas of the sanctuary Sunday after Sunday? While some people have never noticed this pattern, others wish it could change. Why not use this already established pattern, however, as a strength for outreach and caring? Ask someone in each quadrant or section of the sanctuary to be responsible for greeting the visitors that sit in their section. They can do this by always saving enough space on their pew to allow a visitor to come and sit with them. They can personally get to know the visitor and encourage the visitor to leave adequate information on the attendance cards or pad. Moreover, they can engage the visitor in conversation following the service, when many first-time visitors leave quickly since they know no one.

What we are talking about in essence is a sanctuary plan for seating visitors. With such a plan in place, ushers will no longer simply look for the first open area in which to seat visitors. Instead, they will work with a team of other caring members, "sanctuary servants," to find the best place for the visitor to sit. Who are the visitors? Are they single, single with children, married with or without children, older adults, young, middle-aged? If ushers and greeters know who the sanctuary servants are, and where they are seated in the sanctuary, then all can work together in placing visitors with members who have something in common. By seating visitors with compatible sanctuary servants, the ushers will have taken a major step toward meeting the needs of the visitors.

The youth in the church should also be fully included in this whole process of caring for worship visitors. In some churches Boy Scouts and Girl Scouts serve as greeters for a particular worship hour. Scouts are often receptive to this, as it allows them to wear their uniforms and log hours of church and community service toward their merit awards. It also gives the Scouting ministry a high level of public visibility in the total life of the church, instantly appealing to new families with youth who could be involved in Scouting. Likewise, inactive families will sometimes attend worship and find their way back into relationship with the congregation as a result of their daughter's or son's involvement. Perhaps the most important benefit of all is that youth learn the value of being involved in caring for visitors in their congregation and community.

The potential for greeters, ushers, and sanctuary servants to collaborate in ministry is virtually unlimited. Each role is critically important and can make a major difference in helping new and not so new worship visitors feel genuinely welcome and warmly received. The way we respond to our worship visitors has a direct bearing not only on numerical growth, but also on the spiritual health of the congregation.

Older Adults, Shut-ins, the Infirm

Every congregation needs a ministry to its persons physically unable to attend worship. Typically local churches do not excel in meeting the needs of this group with consistency. If visitation occurs on any scheduled basis, only the pastor or someone on the church staff is involved. Part of the vision of Lifestyle Relational Evangelism, however, is to create a visitation team — composed especially of senior members of the congregation — to meet this vital area of need. Congregations can develop a ministry with such persons that is provided primarily by the retired community in its membership. All that is needed is a name, a time, and a plan. One of the original LRE congregations named its group the "Calling and Caring Ministry." This group began meeting weekly on a weekday morning at 10:00 at the church building. Their plan is to share in a time of gathering, then to assign everyone to a ministry team to go out and make calls on persons confined to their homes. After the calls are made on each day of visitation, the entire group meets for lunch together at a local restaurant. This provides an opportunity for the teams to share what they have learned or experienced during the visits, and to inform everyone else in the ministry of the ongoing needs of the homebound and elderly.

Consider how wonderful a ministry like this can be for these persons in our congregations who are often the loneliest and most "invisible" members of the congregation. They desperately desire fellowship and caring, yet all too often the demands on church staff do not allow adequate time for this type of calling. Some persons desire to be visited once a week, others less frequently. With a Calling and Caring ministry in place, these needs can be met regularly throughout the year. The members of a Calling and Caring Ministry, in turn, will experience blessings beyond imagination as they reach out and touch the lives of others.

This has been one of the most rewarding ministries I have ever been associated with as a pastor. I have seen many persons reached, befriended, and lifted out of loneliness. I have seen others who thought of themselves as homebound begin to consider living again as they watched (and were visited by) friends who seemed far less able to be out and about than they. I have marveled to see persons who thought they were homebound take courage, become part of the visitation effort, and join the fellowship of the meal each week. Perhaps the most profound example I have ever known is one many across the country have come to know as "Mama Waunette."

When I first heard of Waunette she was described to me as a wonderful Christian woman who had some serious health problems and was able to get out only rarely. I decided to go and visit her. My first couple of calls with her were very pleasant and enjoyable. She had a beautiful spirit and was a joyful hostess to all who came into her home. She had a gift of making people feel welcome. She shared with me that the Lord had blessed her life in many ways but that many in the community and in the congregation had advised her not to get out much because of her health problems. I asked her about the possibility of starting a weekly Bible study and sharing group in her home. She responded warmly to this offer and we began a couple of weeks later.

As Waunette and I grew closer, I realized that she had a dynamic witness that needed to be heard. Others had convinced her, however, that she should not get out. We prayed together and asked the Lord to give her a new vision of how the Spirit could use her in ministry. We discussed the LRE ministry that had begun in the congregation. She said she wished there was some way she could participate, and we discussed possibilities. More prayers went up daily about this lovely woman.

One morning as I was eating breakfast with her at her house, she seemed excited about life in a way I had not noticed before. She explained to me that the Lord had told her to get out more. Then she said, "Jim, with Jesus' help, I am going to give up being a shut-in. I want to be involved in ministry for Christ, not only through Bible study but also through visitation."

I could hardly contain myself. I was witnessing the transformation of another life for Christ. Members of the LRE ministry began bringing Waunette to visitation on Thursday nights. She went out to knock on doors in the community. Then, with Waunette's support and enthusiasm, we began a Calling and Caring Ministry to the homebound. On Thursday nights we began to call Waunette "Mama," because she rallied us on to new heights of ministry. She would tell people, "If I can do it, you know you can in the Lord."

When we were first invited to go to the California-Nevada Conference, she was thrilled for us. She informed me over lunch one day that she would be praying for the team as we prepared to make that long trip. She also told me that she had never been on a jet before in her life. One week later, as I was finalizing the trip list for reservations, she told me that she had decided to go with us. She said she had prayed it through and knew the Lord wanted her to go. I remember the courage I saw in her joyful face as she walked onto that Delta L-10-11 jet at the Atlanta airport. She was anxious, but she was doing what the Lord had called her to do. She did fine on the flight and that night in California she surprised us all.

Though many of us had shared our testimonies publicly, Waunette had never done this before. She nudged me as I prepared to address an almost full sanctuary, "If you need me to share, I am ready to try. The Lord has given me something to say." I called on her that night and, as she steadily made her way to the pulpit, we all stood in amazement. She gave one of the most glowing testimonies I have ever heard. As a result of her testimony I saw tears fall, hearts melt, and lives experience transformation; God was present in this woman who had retired from being a shut-in.

Waunette went on from there to travel with the LRE ministry nearly everywhere we went. Her mailbox was often filled with letters from persons from across the U.S.A. whose lives had been touched by the Lord through her. Now in her eighties, she still visits in her local church, shares new victories in her life, and has a ready testimony for her Lord. We will never be the same because of her life.

Waunette is a wonderful example of how members of the retired community can provide ministry in a way that no one else can. Many of these persons have time to give and need an avenue of genuine ministry in the local church. An LRE ministry to older adults and homebound persons has worked well in other congregations; one can work in your congregation, too.

Only God knows how many others are out there in our local churches and communities today waiting to be touched by the ministry of LRE, or invited to participate in it. The horizons of LRE can be expanded in many directions. Ministry, such as "Calling and Caring" described above, can be expanded to include visitation in local nursing homes and hospitals for members and relatives of members (see *What Do You Say?* and *Nursing Home Worship*, Discipleship Resources). Further, those doing visitation and those being visited are not the only ones blessed through LRE. Families and friends are also touched when they see the local church begin to consistently care for their relatives and friends. Be creative. Have an open heart. Reach out to others. Go out beyond the walls. Press on!

❖ 4. Getting Started

The first step in starting a ministry of LRE is to know the congregation and its needs. Without proper background and preparation — not only in the theory of LRE but also in the history and situation of the congregation — an initial group of well-meaning leaders can unintentionally misrepresent the nature of LRE. As a result, the congregation may misunderstand or misinterpret the purpose of the ministry. Is LRE a massive agenda imposed on the local church by a few leaders? Is it designed to make the entire congregation tow a certain line of thought? This is *not* what LRE is about, but leaders must know their congregation in order to communicate what LRE really is.

Realistic Beginnings

It is infinitely better to start small with a few excellent commitments than to start large with poor commitments. Inspiration can have a positive effect on us in the church, but we cannot run solely on inspiration. LRE is long-haul ministry. It is not a quick fix to a short-range problem. Typically, an LRE ministry will begin with one or two laypersons who have learned about the ministry and are committed to seeing it work in their congregation. Members of United Methodist Men's groups have successfully sponsored LRE in many congregations. (Special instructions for United Methodist Men groups are included in Appendix A.) Members of other groups — United Methodist Women, a Sunday school class, or simply a few committed friends — can also sponsor LRE. Two people in the beginning is fine. That is twice as good as only one!

With a team of two or perhaps three in place, the next step is prayer. Prayer is a key to the effectiveness of all ministries; LRE is no exception. Pray together about the congregation — its struggles, conflicts, hopes, and opportunities. As you pray, begin talking about the possibilities of LRE with an ever-widening circle of members, including the pastor. Invite each one to read this book. Pray diligently as prayer partners, but begin immediately to involve as many others as possible in prayer for the development of this ministry.

As your group of interest and support begins to grow, the initial leaders will need to meet in person with the pastor. Invite the pastor to read this book. Give the pastor a personal copy to keep in his or her library to refer to as the ministry develops. Most important, seek the prayer support of the pastor for this undertaking. Pastors need to know that LRE is in the best interests of the entire congregation.

At the initial meeting with your pastor, you will want to emphasize that LRE is biblical in content and Wesleyan in theology. Communicate clearly that LRE is a national program of United Methodist Men. It is published by the General Board of Discipleship of The United Methodist Church and endorsed by the Evangelism staff of the Board. It is *not* a high pressure visitation program. Put the emphasis where this book puts it — on building relationships, meeting needs, and trusting God with the long-term spiritual results.

Even with these assurances, pastors may still have some suggestions about how to enhance the ministry — and rightly so. Work with your pastor in thinking about ways the LRE emphases can dovetail with the already existing ministries of the congregation. Don't be afraid to innovate, but don't be afraid to collaborate either.

As the initial leaders gain actual experience in ministry, plan weekly informal meetings to share the joys and discoveries of LRE with your pastor. You have no idea how supportive such reports can be to your pastor. Also keep the pastor informed as new relationships develop through LRE. At some point your pastor will probably want to be included in this ministry. You can invite your pastor early on, but do not place pressure on him or her to participate on a regular basis. Use discernment in this area.

After the pastor has been informed and brought on board as much as possible, the initial leaders can begin in earnest to recruit others for training. As you move into the recruiting process, a number of things will begin happening at once — for example, talking with recruits, spreading the word about LRE throughout the congregation, planning for a specific training model (see Appendix B). We shall discuss each of these steps in more detail. First, however, we must take one point that is already implied above and make it absolutely clear.

Let me state this point as simply and directly as possible: *The initial leaders of LRE should already be involved in the actual practice of visitation before they recruit others to become involved.* Too often, in the church, we invite people to get involved in ministry when we ourselves have yet to step out in faith. As a result, we are not really in a position to train those who respond to our invitation. We do not want this to happen to LRE. If you are one of the initial leaders, you will want to have completed all of the steps outlined above, including the experience of making calls in the field *before you recruit others.* Your experience will provide an important perspective from which to share, pray, and invite others into training. The entire recruiting process will gain integrity, insight, and spiritual power as a result of your experience.

Putting Together a Spiritual Team

Recruiting others to join in ministry is a major and exciting part of LRE. People can become involved in LRE at many different entry points and they can grow spiritually at many different levels. LRE is completely cross-generational. Young people mix well with older and middle-aged adults for the purposes of this ministry. This could be one of the few ministries to encourage persons of all ages and both sexes to blend together for team ministry. LRE differs from some other kinds of evangelism ministries in this respect. Very few ministries are really open to all members of the congregation. LRE is a spiritual program in which persons experience a tremendous bonding with one another as a result of being in ministry together.

There are, however, some basic guidelines that you should follow prayerfully in order to be an effective recruiter. These have been discovered through the experience of many congregations; they lead to powerful ministry.

1. *Share testimonies with the congregation about the joys and discoveries of LRE, but recruit people one at a time.* Keep your congregation informed about how the ministry is developing. Invite everyone to pray for those who are getting involved. Likewise, explain that anyone who wants to join the visitation training is welcome, but do not

appeal for deep commitments publicly. Rationale: Nothing awakens the spiritual vitality of a congregation more than the opportunity to hear about how God is working in the lives of other laypersons. This kind of sharing keeps the church alive and fresh. Without it, we fall prey to preservers of the mundane. Nothing is more of a wet blanket, however, than general appeals for volunteers. Many have volunteered before and have burned out. The most meaningful invitations are grounded in prayer and conveyed individually.

2. *Always recruit in person, never over the telephone.* It is best not to even mention your desire to recruit someone until you are really ready to sit down and talk about what is involved. Rationale: People have many stereotypes about what outreach evangelism is. If you start them thinking about their stereotypes ahead of time, you will have a much more difficult time describing a true picture of LRE.

3. *Do not get caught in the trap of trying to recruit large numbers of people for your first training event.* Let interested individuals come to you as a result of your public sharing before the congregation, or prayerfully seek out only those you feel led to recruit. If you start with two leaders, your first series of training sessions might increase by only two trainees. Rationale: It is far better to start with a small number who are absolutely committed than with a roomful of bodies who have a low level of commitment.

4. *Always pray diligently for the person you are going to recruit before you ever talk with him or her.* Be as sure as you can in your own heart that the Spirit is leading you specifically to this person. If you have this kind of confidence, share this when you talk with the person. Let him or her know of the affirmation that you have received in prayer. If you do not receive spiritual affirmation, do not go to see this person. Keep praying. Rationale: God builds this ministry and perpetuates it with the Spirit, not with our personalities.

5. *Let the Lord use you to create a spiritual vision of LRE so that the recruit sees the joy, adventure, and privilege of becoming involved.* This is not just another program. The recruit is not "helping you out" by doing this. This is a holy calling; the spiritual course of lives hangs in the balance. The Holy Spirit will use those involved in LRE and will transform them through their involvement in this ministry. Nothing is more joyful than to know that God has directly used us to touch another life. Communicate this vision with crystal clarity. Rationale: People are bored with more of the same in church. Here is a ministry that is mandated by God. It is not like anything they have ever experienced.

6. *Do not take an answer from the recruit immediately, whether it be no or yes.* Ask the recruit to pray about his or her involvement in the ministry and to consider trying it for a time. Any time people perceive us as being pushy, insistent, or impatient, we communicate desperation. People do not like to associate with desperadoes. LRE is, above all, a patient ministry; it waits on God's timing. Be sensitive. Listen to the recruit's concerns. You are giving an invitation from Christ; the response is also to him, not to you. Rationale: The motivation of those who enter into the training must come from Christ, not from the recruiters. Being motivated by Christ will make all the difference in the quality of a person's witness.

7. *Make it clear to prospective recruits that LRE is a long-term ministry of excellence.* Our primary responsibility is to be faithful, not to get results. <u>Results are left strictly to the Holy Spirit.</u> Our faithfulness in going out is within our control. Results are in God's control. We will often plant seeds and never see them grow. Still, we rejoice in the opportunity to be servants of Christ in reaching out to others in his name and Spirit. Rationale: Too many persons are looking for a quick fix and want instant gratification based simply on numerical results. The church did not lose its spiritual role in society overnight. We will recover a little at a time — in God's time, provided we are faithful. Excellence does not come quickly.

Recruiting is one of the most rewarding experiences we can have in the ministry of LRE. Seeing a family that is relatively uninvolved in ministry coming into the fullness of ministry brings tremendous joy. We know that God not only uses us to reach out to the lost and the inactives but to call disciples, who will in turn multiply our efforts as a church. Pray, plan, recruit; then move out beyond the walls.

5. Organizing Teams

Teams of caring visitors are the lifeblood of LRE ministry. Consider well: The spiritual promise of LRE will never reach most of the people in the ministry area of your congregation unless it flows through the hearts and minds of a well-defined and well-trained team. Training is not, therefore, something that can happen haphazardly or in the abstract. Training requires getting down to specific decisions such as who should be on a team, where the team will visit, when the team will visit, and how they will conduct themselves as they visit. These are the questions that guide this and the next two chapters.

Someone might ask, "Why do we need *teams*? LRE is about building relationships and meeting needs; what do teams add to these actions that individual members of the congregation cannot accomplish on their own?" Much of the reasoning behind the use of teams will become clear as we proceed. Just here, however, a summary answer may be helpful.

The focus of team ministry in this chapter has to do with going out into the community on a *regular* basis in order to visit in *every* home, to discover who people are, and how your congregation may be able to serve them on a *long-term* basis. In this light, teams do not replace or compete with the motivation of individual Christians to *live* the spiritual vision of LRE at all times and in all places. Rather, teams give congregations a systematic way of responding to the needs of their total ministry area. Apart from a team strategy, individual members will not be able to reach the total ministry area in an effective way. Simply put, teams make it possible for a congregation to relate itself to its surrounding community in a way that most fully, responsibly, and accountably embodies the spiritual vision of LRE.

Who Is on a Team?

As the result of literally thousands of visitation calls, LRE congregations have discovered that the most effective teams have certain characteristics. In the first place, teams are ideally composed of three persons. One person serves as the *designated team leader*. He or she is the one responsible for conducting the visit. This person guides the conversation and keeps the visit moving. He or she also makes the primary decisions about where the team will go once it enters the field.

The second person on the team is a *support person*. This person observes carefully and listens closely to what happens during the visit. He or she also participates in the conversations in a natural way, but the primary task is to be attentive to things that may not be obvious on the surface. People will not often directly share their deepest needs, though they may hint at them indirectly. Sometimes clues in the room, as well as words exchanged, may tell a story about the family being visited. The support person remains alert to these indirect clues with spiritual eyes and ears.

The third member of the team is the *recorder*. This person takes notes during the visit, then fills out the appropriate administrative forms (see Chapter 7) after returning to the church building. This person carries a small clipboard (preferably a 6" x 9" size) with notepaper for writing, as well as the necessary forms, and perhaps a brochure or other information about the congregation to hand out. The recorder can also participate in the conversation, but his or her most important task is to listen and make notes. Naturally the recorder should never write down anything on the forms except the requested basic information (see Chapter 7). Certainly, no information of a confidential nature should be recorded in writing.

Persons new to visitation ministry may fear at first that the presence of a recorder will give offense. Won't those being visited resent the idea of someone taking notes during the conversation? A new team member once even suggested that people might suspect the team of "casing" the house for criminal activity. These objections, however, have emerged only in the minds of persons anxious about going on a visit. In over 4,000 visits, I have yet to hear of anyone who was upset by the presence of the recorder. Some people may ask what you are writing. In this case, simply show the visitation form and explain its purpose — to get to know the people, and to keep track of how the congregation may be able to serve. If these matters are shared openly and honestly, suspicion is not likely to creep in. Some people have even volunteered to fill out the form themselves.

As you think about sharing in ways that are open and honest, consider also the importance of body language. The way we communicate with others is always influenced by the language of our bodies. There are many theories about body language. Some say that crossed arms indicate defensiveness. Others say that clasped hands indicate being tense. Regardless of the theory, LRE teams should make it their aim to communicate a sense of being at ease — whatever that *naturally* is for each of us.

Consider, for example, where teams stand or sit during a visit. Visiting outside, or on the front porch, is entirely acceptable. Don't feel that you have to go into someone's home to have an effective visit. Whether you sit or stand, however, a few guidelines will help team members fulfill their different roles. As the leader of conversation, the team leader should always take a position closest to the head(s) of the household. The support person should be next closest, and then the recorder, whose role is to take notes and observe. This may feel a bit mechanical for the first few visits, but it will become a natural part of team body language after several visits in the field.

How team members sit or stand is also important. Sitting on the edge of your seat can communicate uneasiness; standing at a distance, uncertainty. Likewise, crowding a doorway when you first knock can communicate pushiness. In any of these instances, your visit may begin in a recovery mode. Therefore, it is important when standing or taking a seat to do so as though you were at your best friend's home. Be obviously comfortable. Sit back and relax. Stand at ease. Most especially, be yourself and enjoy the experience. You are there to represent Christ. He loves these people. That is also your purpose.

Still another consideration in the composition of teams is the placement and distribution of men and women. LRE visitation is not only open to both men and women, it is conscientious that both should be involved. Without a balance of men and women on each team, your visitation ministry could prove lopsided. Experience has shown, furthermore, that every team needs at least one woman. Simply put, the presence of a woman is reassuring to most people. Imagine yourself answering the door in the evening and finding three strange men on your doorstep. We also recommend that the woman be the team leader where possible. Some of the finest team leaders in the field today are women.

What about husbands, wives, and singles? Some team members may be married, while others may be single. Generally, we do not make a practice of placing husbands and wives on the same team. This seems to stifle the willingness of either to open up to strangers. In most marriages, one partner is more outgoing in personality than the other. The more passive spouse may allow his or her more assertive partner to carry the weight of conversation, especially when placed in a new situation. We don't want this in LRE. Ideally, each member of the team should feel the freedom to participate and to share openly. Therefore, generally, we do not suggest sending husbands and wives out on the same ministry team.

Children and youth can also be active in LRE visitation. Many churches have young persons who want to go visiting with the adults and are a valuable part of the ministry. Young people are natural at meeting new friends. They do not come into LRE carrying the same negative stereotypes and reservations about evangelism that adults often bring. They are much less likely to worry about being rejected, embarrassed, or placed in an uncomfortable position than the adults. We can learn much in these areas from our children and young people who go visiting with us. Likewise, our sensitivity and affirmation will help them grow through this ministry — both in their sense of commitment to the church and in seeing themselves as a significant part of the church's ministry.

In this light, we should register another advantage of team ministry: Teams are an irreplaceable means of support for their members. Certainly scripture supports the wisdom and appropriateness of being part of a team. According to Matthew 6:7, Jesus "called the twelve and began to send them out two by two, and gave them authority over the unclean spirits" (Mark 6:7). As Christians, we work better alongside others in the faith than we do solo. We are much more likely to continue in faithfulness when we are part of a team dedicated to a cause than when we are out on our own trying to do what we think needs doing. Likewise, if the members of the team face conflict — which they sometimes will — they can encourage one another. Teams share good times as well as bad times together. Team members can lift each other in prayer when one or the other is down or when things are not going well. For all of these reasons, visitation is a team effort; it is not something that anyone should normally do alone.

At the same time, some cautions should be observed. These guidelines are not intended to cover every situation. Each ministry is unique; some things work better in some places than others. For example, some LRE teams are limited to only two members; two can still conduct an effective visit. On the other hand, LRE congregations have found that it is never wise to visit with more than three members on a team. Four or more is simply too many bodies invading someone's home. A four-person team will usually make those being visited feel uncomfortable or even pressured. Think about how you might feel if four strangers came to your door.

In essence, ministry teams are designed to be *consistent caring units* of the local church. They are not out in the field to look for spiritual scalps or enhanced statistics. They go into ministry areas in order to serve, to love, to care, to be the church in the world, and to do all of this on an *ongoing* basis. In order to do this in the best way, however, they need one another, and they need an organized way to identify their ministry area.

Where Do Teams Visit?

Every local church is surrounded by a parish. Some congregations claim a large neighborhood as their parish; others focus on a small area of dense population. In yet other cases, the parish of the congregation may be made up of persons from distant geographical locations around a rural or metropolitan area. The ministry of Lifestyle Relational Evangelism is compatible with any of these parish settings.

The most important principle to establish in relation to ministry area has little to do with the kind of parish your congregation claims. It has everything to do with a simple question: *Are you as a congregation willing to relate yourself to your local community?* This may seem an obvious question; but the answer is not nearly so obvious when we look at the actual practice of many congregations. In far too many cases, congregations are surrounded by unchurched people in their communities, but the congregations themselves have forgotten how to reach out into these communities with spiritual compassion and vision. The principle that needs to be lifted up is also simple:

**The spiritual health of a congregation is revealed in its willingness
to relate itself to its immediate community.**

What is the best way for a congregation to relate itself to its surrounding community? LRE congregations have found that one of the best methods is to provide teams with maps of specific ministry areas. Teams need to know where they are going; they also need to keep track of where they have been. Likewise, various teams need to know what other teams are learning and doing in the total ministry area of the congregation: Where are relationships flourishing with new people? Where do members of other congregations live? Has someone on a particular street requested that no further visitors be sent to his or her house? These are all matters that can be tracked on a map.

The first step is to acquire a detailed map of the area surrounding your congregation. One can acquire a quality map at nearly any city or county courthouse in the United States. Such official maps may be expensive to obtain if you have to order them through a blue-print company, but for a small fee, courthouse personnel may be able to make copies. These kinds of maps show the location of every house and lot on every street. Builders, real estate agents, and lawyers use them to keep track of property lines and easements. An example of this type of map appears on the following page.

Once you have acquired a detailed map, the next step is to study it. Where do current members live? How far out does the current membership extend in terms of geographic area? How much of the surrounding area could your congregation minister to effectively? Think in realistic yet optimistic terms, and draw a circle around the *total ministry area* of your congregation as you currently see it. As you gain experience with LRE, you may later want to expand your vision.

Once you have identified the total ministry area, the next step is to divide this area up into *team ministry areas*. A team ministry area is the specified area in which a particular team will visit. Each team has *one* ministry area. An exception here, of course, would be a team that is designed for a special visitation group — for example, seniors visiting with shut-ins. Such special teams are identified less by area than by the group they serve. For general ministry teams reaching out to unchurched families, however, the goal is to have one team in each area, and for each team to visit eventually with *every* person in its ministry area.

An example of a Platt map used for community visitation.

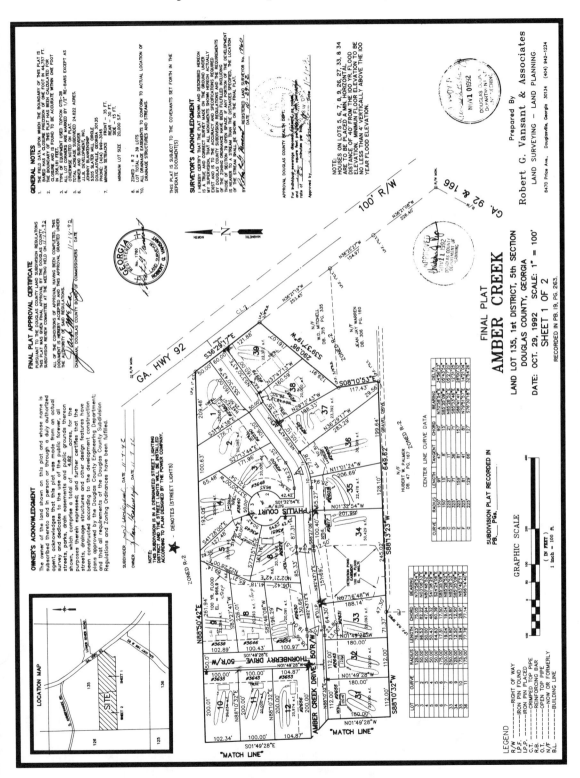

Platt map supplied by Gerald Vansant of Robert G. Vansant & Associates, Douglasville, GA.

In many cases, you will discover that team ministry areas are unique in several ways. For one thing, team areas can often be identified simply by observing various neighborhood borders and natural boundaries. For example, you may want to draw boundaries on your map around subdivisions, housing developments, city blocks, county roads, rivers, quadrants, or other obvious dividing lines. Many of these bounded areas will tend to have a distinct personality depending on the people who live there and the history of how the area has developed. Teams serving in these areas will also develop their own unique styles of ministry and visitation tuned to the needs of each area.

As you think about team members, furthermore, you may want to consider placing teams according to where members already live, if at all possible. Such placement can enhance the ability of the team members to see their area as their own parish. Teams will tend to do this in any event, but living in the area of ministry may enable them to have more contact with those receiving ministry. In a real sense, the persons on the teams serve as lay pastors, meeting and caring for their new flocks whom they have met by knocking on doors in the name of the church and the Risen Christ.

As a result of having a bounded area in which to serve, team members will grow closer to each other and to those they are called to serve. Teams will discover some persons who are actively involved in another local congregation. They will discover others who have special long-term needs. They will also discover some whose only reaction to the church is one of anger and rejection. In all of this, teams can grow in discernment and ministry in many ways.

The subject of ministry area is also a good place to locate the issue of dress code. What should team members wear as they go out to visit? Will they dress in their Sunday finest? Or will they go in sloppy clothes as though preparing to do yardwork? Neither of these two extremes is usually advisable. As with the subject of body language, the key to attire is to be at home in your ministry area. Pay attention to the ministry area itself. How are the people you visit likely to be dressed? Try to fit in, rather than stand out. Never allow wardrobe to become an obstacle to making others feel comfortable.

As a rule of thumb, LRE teams have found that casual clothing serves best for most situations. For men, a pair of slacks and a nice shirt with an open collar may be suitable. For women, pants and a blouse or a casual dress seem to be generally ideal. In any case, wardrobe should never become a major issue. Being at ease for the sake of building relationships is the key to this as to many other decisions.

Teams will naturally follow up on persons who indicate a clear interest in building a relationship. This is true whether or not those visited decide to attend Sunday school or worship. Likewise, team members can rejoice in the presence of members of other congregations, and they can commit themselves to pray for and remain open to those who reject them. The goal of every team visit should be that those visited will know that they have experienced church in their own home.

Above all, using designated ministry areas gives teams the opportunity to *be* the church. As we keep emphasizing, LRE requires patience, hope, love, and wisdom; a team area gives focus, discipline, and accountability to these virtues. LRE teams are called to meet others as friends, to discover their needs, and to minister to them at that point. This is the most powerful witness of Christian love.

When Do Teams Visit?

With any ministry of a lasting nature, those involved must consider how the ministry develops over time. In Chapter 7 we shall look in detail at how teams can keep track of whom they have visited, how many times they have visited, and when it may be appropriate to visit again. In order to make the best use of time, however, another matter must be settled first.

What time of day or week is the best time to visit? If you have been reading carefully, you will have realized by now that there is no single correct answer to this question. LRE is a way of life centered on building relationships and meeting needs. Visiting in this way can happen at any time — during the day or during the evening, on weekends or weekdays. As we mentioned in Chapter 3, moreover, some LRE teams may have a special time slot due either to the constituency of the team members (older adults visiting the homebound on a weekday morning — see page 29) or to the characteristics of those being visited (worship visitors should be contacted within the first twenty-four to forty-eight hours after they have attended worship — see page 27). Apart from these special considerations, however, and in order to enhance the power of working together and learning from each other, the majority of your LRE ministry teams should schedule regular visitation for a specific evening each week.

LRE congregations have generally found that a specific evening of the week is best for team visitation. This is, of course, a natural concession to the daytime work schedules of most people (both visitors and those being visited). Congregations are not unanimous, however, on which night of the week is best. Something might be said in favor of avoiding weekend evenings, as these are frequently times when families do things together. On the other hand, don't forget that some people may feel very alone and isolated, especially on weekends. Likewise, something might be said for visiting earlier in the week — say, on Mondays, Tuesdays, or Wednesdays — as this gives people an opportunity to consider whether or not they want to attend worship or Sunday school on the following Sunday. All other factors being equal, however, many LRE congregations have found that Thursday night is the best night for midweek visitation.

Visiting on Thursday evenings has several advantages. For one thing, in keeping with the above, having had a good solid visit early in the evening on Thursday gives people an opportunity to consider the place of church in their plans for the weekend. People generally begin to think about their weekends on Thursday nights before going to work on Fridays. Families can talk together about their options. Also, most people are at home on Thursday evenings. Many civic organizations hold their meetings on Monday or Tuesday night, and Wednesday nights are often already scheduled with other church activities. For all of these reasons, Thursday is the best evening for visitation in many congregations.

The need to select a specific evening for regular team visitation becomes even more compelling when we consider the elements that make up the evening itself. As we have been saying all along, one of the real advantages of team ministry is the way the teams and team members learn from each other. On a typical visitation evening, teams have several opportunities for this kind of mutual support and instruction. Again, there are no hard and fast rules, but a typical evening might look as follows:

6:30 P.M.	Gathering at the church in the map room
6:40	Assignment of teams and areas
6:50	Group prayer and sending out
7:00-8:20	Time spent in the field
8:20-8:30	Filling out forms and completing correspondence
8:30-8:45	Report Session and Festival of Praise

Notice several things about this schedule. First, everyone begins and ends together in fellowship and prayer. Teams are not always eager to go out. Likewise, some teams return after what may seem an uneventful evening. In faith, however, we know that no attempt to reach out to others is uneventful. We know and believe that everything we do can be used by the Lord for his honor and glory. The results are up to God and we simply celebrate faithfulness in going. We share with one another before we go into the field, then we celebrate faithfulness together when we return to the church building.

This format also encourages accountability. Each person receives assignments and reports on the attempt of his or her team to carry out the assignments. Sometimes assignments can be completed; at other times, they cannot. The point, however, is that we are together in our efforts, and we celebrate our efforts in Christ. Someone in the group is going to have a divine appointment. Someone is going to be blessed in a special way. This will be shared with the entire group. As a result, all teams will begin to see lives change for God. In this way, LRE team meetings become a powerful reminder to all: Be patient and trust God in all things; the Spirit can and will use you to minister to others.

As a result of team meetings such as this, you can expect to see a remarkable closeness to Christ and to one another emerge in your LRE ministry. Hearts will be strangely warmed and faith will steadily grow stronger. The Lord will reveal himself in new and wonderful ways. All will see the hand of the Lord at work through this ministry. Lives will never be the same. To be sure, this bonding will take time and commitment on the part of all visitation team members, but team members should know in their hearts that someone in the ministry area will have a first encounter with Christ as a result of their willingness to visit. With this thought dwelling in the heart, no one will have to be pressured to come to visitation. Indeed, each will discover his or her own motivation through the love of the Risen Christ! This motivation is unstoppable. Believe, commit, trust, train teams, and move out beyond the walls.

❖ 6. The Great Adventure of Visitation

Visiting the people in your ministry area with your LRE team is a great adventure. Like all adventures, however, visitation requires imagination. Having read to this point, you have already begun to think about the neighborhoods around your congregation (your neighborhood!) as a ministry area. If you are part of an LRE training event, you may also have discovered by now who some of your team members are. Perhaps you have begun to picture yourself with your team on an actual visit. Have you pictured yourself standing at someone's front door, or sitting in someone's living room? Have you thought about what you might want to say? How would you dress for the occasion? What impression would you want to make on people during the first visit? How might the focus of your relationships change after, say, five visits?

Naturally, no one can answer all of these questions in a way that predicts the responses of a living situation. Indeed, this is what makes visitation such a great adventure. As you go out with your team, you do not know exactly how people will respond. All you know for sure is that you will be there to offer genuine friendship, to build relationships, to meet needs, and to serve Christ in any way that you can.

Still, it is possible to imagine (and helpful to anticipate) some of the different kinds of things that may happen as you go out to visit in the Spirit of our Lord. In the remainder of this chapter, we shall look at three different visitation settings: first-time visit, follow-up visit, and casual acquaintance visit. We shall try to get inside a "typical" first-time visit and a casual acquaintance visit by means of two dramatic dialogues. That's right; we shall listen in on some hypothetical conversations between visitors and persons being visited. In each case, moreover, we shall review the dialogues for signs of how they try to embody the spiritual vision of LRE.

These dialogues and comments are not intended to be the last word. LRE *is* truly an adventure. As you read through these materials, you may disagree with my inferences and comments about the scripted dialogues. You may feel that the hypothetical team would have been wiser and truer to the Spirit of Christ to take a different tack. That will be alright. All of us must follow the light we are given as we respond to the presence and needs of others. Follow the promptings of the Holy Spirit in your own heart. Share your feelings and insights with the members of your team. Listen and learn from others. That is what the great adventure of Lifestyle Relational Evangelism is all about.

First-Time Visit

Bill, Jim, and Mary are a visitation team from their local church. They are assigned to the Red Rock subdivision, a relatively new housing area of 120 homes in a developing part of the county. Bill has been in the congregation for most of his life. Jim is a new member of only four months. Mary is a member of three years who teaches Sunday school. The name of their congregation is First United Methodist of Rockledge.

Before leaving the church building to go to their new ministry area, the team members decide that Bill will be their team leader. Mary is recognized as the support person, and Jim will serve as the recorder. All three feel comfortable in these roles, so they decide that this will be their normal team composition. Before leaving the church, Jim makes sure he has all the necessary forms and materials to use during their time in the ministry area — initial visit forms, doorknockers, brochures about the congregation, recent newsletters, etc. They join with all of the other teams in a time of prayer before they hit the street.

As they enter the Red Rock development, they decide to ride through the area comparing how the streets are laid out in comparison to the map of the subdivision. This helps them to become familiar with the general layout of their ministry area. They notice several things as they drive around:

- The presence or absence of children and children's toys, bikes, etc.
- The general appearance of the homes and yards. Are they well cared for and neat? Or are they run down in appearance and uncared for?
- What kinds of cars are in the yards and carports? What other vehicles or things are in the yards, such as boats, motorcycles, etc.?
- Which houses were built here first? Is one section of this area newer than another? Are the homes all of the same type?

Bill, Mary, and Jim kid each other as they realize that they are asking the same kinds of questions real estate agents ask. They are also aware, however, that their purpose is quite different from real estate speculation. This is going to be their ministry area; they need to know it well in order to relate effectively to the people who live here.

Once they have developed a basic sense of the layout and atmosphere of their new ministry area, they begin to look for a place to make their first visit. They see a man working in his yard. The man is making an island of pine straw in one small section of the yard near the driveway. They stop the car and get out on the street. They approach the yard. As they walk up the driveway, the man notices them coming to see him.

Bill: *(Now close to the man)* Hello there. We're from First United Methodist Church here in Rockledge, and we're out getting to know people in Red Rock. We thought we would stop to visit with you for a minute if that's O.K.

Man: *(Looking a little tense, but leaning on his rake)* Well, at least you're not with those Jehovah's Witnesses who show up here about once every couple of weeks. I should warn you though, we're Baptists.

Bill: *(Smiling cordially)* Yes, I know what you mean about the Jehovah's Witnesses; they can be persistent, can't they? By the way, my name is Bill *(reaches out to shake hands)* and this is Jim and Mary. *(Everyone shakes hands.)*

Man: *(Returning a courteous smile)* Well, my name is Dick Reeves; it's nice to meet you.

Bill: Well, Dick, I'm glad to know that you and your family are Baptist, but we're not out to see if we can meet only Methodists. We're out to get to know the people of our community and to make new friends.

Dick: Well, that's fine. I mean we all want to meet new friends, but we've been Baptist for a long time.

Mary: I know what you mean, Dick. My husband and I were Baptist for nearly twenty years before coming to Rockledge, and we have friends who attend First Baptist in Rockledge. In fact, the Baptists and Methodists here in Rockledge have been known to work together on joint mission projects. By the way, Dick, how long have you and your family lived here?

Dick: We've been here about a month. We moved here from Columbia, South Carolina, due to a transfer from work. I work for American Data Corporation. It was a good promotion for me, but it's just not the same as South Carolina. We knew so many more people back there.

Jim: Say, I had a roommate in college who was from South Carolina. He's still a good friend. He's also a fanatical Gamecock football fan! *(Jim had noticed a Gamecock decal on Dick's truck when the team walked into the driveway.)*

Dick: *(Grinning)* Oh, yes. I know all about those Gamecocks. I guess I'm one of their strongest supporters. Are you football fans, too?

Bill: *(Enthusiastic)* Oh, yes. Our congregation seems to be full of fans. Mostly from Georgia Tech, but our pastor is an old Georgia Bulldog supporter.

Dick: You don't say! Well, I don't have anything good to say about those slobbering dogs. I don't see how you can even listen to him preach, knowing he's a Bulldog fan! Ha! Won't you come on inside and meet my wife and have a glass of tea or something?

Bill: Well, we don't want to keep you from your work.

Dick: Don't worry about that. I was dreading doing this today anyway. Come on in, won't you?

Bill: Sure. We'd be glad to. *(They all go inside and stand in the foyer to the living room.)*

Dick: *(Very friendly now)* Please have a seat anywhere. Make yourselves at home and let me go get Cindy. *(He goes off down the hall, and then returns.)* Folks, this is my wife, Cindy. *(Then, speaking to Cindy)* I was just outside and these folks came up and we began to talk. They're from First Methodist here in Rockledge.

Cindy: *(Smiling, but reserved)* Hello, nice to meet you.

Mary: Well, Cindy, are you about to get settled in?

Cindy: I don't think I ever will. I mean, this is the first time we've moved away from where both of our families live and it just seems impossible to get things like they were before.

Mary: I know just what you mean. When we moved here from New Jersey we thought we'd never get settled again. But after meeting new friends and getting to know people in our neighborhood and at church, our house began to feel more like home.

Dick: Well, would anyone care for a cold soda or a glass of tea or something?

Bill: Sure, I'll have some ice water.

Mary: I think I'll pass this time. I just had supper a little while ago.

Jim: A glass of tea would be fine for me, thanks. *(Dick leaves to prepare the drinks for everyone.)*

Bill: Well, Cindy, this sure is a nice home you have here. I love this style of house with this large great room and all. It looks like it would be very comfortable to live in.

Cindy: *(Smiling)* It is. We got a great deal on it from our real estate company. It's an older home and it seems the previous owners really needed to sell. We really believe God helped us find this house.

Bill: I know what you mean. The Lord has looked out for me in some of the same kinds of ways.

(Dick arrives with the drinks, and Dick and Cindy serve everyone.)

Cindy: Does your church have any groups for women that meet during the daytime?

Bill: Yes, we do. We have a couple of Bible study groups meeting on weekday mornings in different homes in the area. I haven't been involved in one of them personally, but I understand they are really good.

Mary: I have a good friend who doesn't work outside the home and she's in one of them. She loves it and says it's a great bunch of people to get to know.

Cindy: Well, great. Maybe if we come to visit your church I could get you to introduce me to this friend of yours and she could tell me more about the groups.

Dick: That's nice, dear, but I told them that we're Baptists. *(Then, turning to Bill)* I'm sure the First Baptist Church would have something similar, don't you think?

Bill: Oh, I'm sure they probably do. From what some of my friends who go there tell me, it's an active congregation. Have you visited there yet?

Cindy: *(Looking aggravated toward Dick)* It's always next Sunday. I mean, we've talked about it, but we haven't gone yet. We'll probably visit several churches in the area, don't you think, Dick?

Dick: Well, I guess we should, just to be sure where we want to get involved, I mean.

(As this was going on, Mary had looked around the room and noticed some family pictures hanging in one corner.)

Mary: Tell me, Cindy, whose pictures are those over there?

Cindy: Oh. Those are picture of our families. This one is of my Mom and Dad. They're from Columbia and they're getting on in years now. In fact, Dad's going in for tests next week. He's been having dizzy spells and they're not sure why. And this is our daughter who teaches school in Charlotte, North Carolina. She's a graduate of U.S.C.

Mary: What a fine family! I'm sure you both must be very thankful.

Dick: Yes. It's a real blessing to come from a Christian home and to have a closeness with your family.

Bill: Well, I suppose we had better be getting on back to the church now, Dick and Cindy. We certainly have enjoyed meeting you and getting to visit with you tonight. Thanks so much for your hospitality.

Dick and Cindy: We're glad you came.

Bill: *(Now standing up)* Since you mentioned your Dad's dizziness, Cindy, I wonder if you would like for us to pray with you for him before we go.

Cindy: Sure. I would appreciate it.

>   *(Bill leads in prayer as everyone holds hands.)*

Jim: Say, Dick, I meant to tell you that our church sends out a monthly newsletter we'd be glad to send you if I can get your address. *(Dick gives the address to him.)*

Bill: And, Cindy, if you'll give me your telephone number, I'll ask my friend Pam to call you about the Bible studies if you wish. We'd also like to call and check on your dad.

Cindy: *(No hesitation)* Sure. It's 355-2716. Thanks for thinking of it.

Bill: We've certainly enjoyed meeting you and hope to see you again, if not at church then around the neighborhood. *(They all say good-bye.)*

Some might look at this dialogue and draw the conclusion that this was not a very significant visit. The team made no direct presentation of the gospel. Dick and Cindy were not asked to examine the present status of their spiritual journey. From the standpoint of Lifestyle Relational Evangelism, however, this was a tremendous first-time visit with the Reeves family. Let's pause now and underscore a few of the ways in which this is so.

First, *the team met Dick Reeves where he was*, in his yard. They did not expect Dick to stop everything and go inside. Nor did they wait for Dick to visit their congregation before they reached out in an effort to get to know him. The team felt that the casual outdoor setting would be a good place to meet someone and to introduce themselves. Dick's willingness to stop and chat shows that their hunch was well founded.

Second, early on in the visit, Bill *identified the team with a mainstream congregation*, First United Methodist Church of Rockledge. This gave Dick a way to size up the intentions of these strangers who had just entered his yard. Dick was relieved to know that they were not part of one of the cults that had recently badgered him, but he was naturally still unsure what to make of these Methodists. He identified himself as a Baptist, even though (as we later find out) he was not active.

Third, both Bill and Mary chose to *soften the denominational issue in order to keep the conversation on a personal (relational) level*. The team did not really know at that time how important Dick's Baptist background was to him. Was he an active member of a Baptist congregation? Or did he mention this background only because he felt uncomfortable in a conversation with strangers from a church. By affirming his Baptist roots, and turning the conversation back toward more day-to-day kinds of questions, the team members affirmed their genuine interest in Dick and his family, regardless of the denominational background.

Fourth, Jim, the recorder, further reinforced the friendly purpose of the visit by showing a desire to *talk about a less intense, more easygoing subject.* Jim had noticed the home team decal from the University of South Carolina on Dick's truck. Jim felt that a conversation about sports might be a better way for the team members to share something of themselves and to begin to get to know Dick. He was right. At this point, the channels of communication and relationship opened for the first time during the conversation. Finding a common place of interest allowed everyone to relax a little. It allowed Dick, in particular, to feel that he might really want to get to know these people. Only then did he invite Bill, Mary, and Jim to come inside for refreshments and to meet his wife.

Fifth, after meeting Cindy, the team continued to *welcome conversation about the day-to-day concerns of life* — the difficulty of moving, the attractiveness of the Reeves' home, the family pictures, etc. From the standpoint of the LRE team, these topics were not an attempt to break the ice in order to get to the "real" purpose of their visit. These topics were a sensitive way of getting to know the Reeveses, and allowing Dick and Cindy to get to know the team members. The purpose was to build a relationship.

Sixth, as the visit progressed, the *team members were positive about the strengths of their own congregation, and they were positive about the potential of other congregations as well.* Cindy's straightforward question about the availability of groups for women at First U.M.C. is readily answered with helpful information by both Bill and Mary. Bill's and Mary's responses also suggest a kind of openness among the groups at First U.M.C.; neither belongs to one of the groups, but both have friends who do. At the same time, Bill is also open to Dick's follow-up question about the availability of such groups at the Baptist church. Indeed, Bill has friends in the Baptist congregation who speak very highly of their experiences there. (The exchange between Cindy and Dick that followed — about always planning, but never going to church — suggests that Dick was not as concerned with his Baptist roots as his protests implied; but team members did not feel that they had to press this point.)

Seventh, in the normal course of the conversation, team members *were able to identify with a real need and to offer their support to Cindy and Dick.* Mary's interest in the family pictures was another natural focus of conversation for the five people just getting to know each other. Cindy's response concerning her Dad's illness showed that she was open to the potential for genuine friendship and support. In light of both Dick's and Cindy's affirmation of their Christian heritage, moreover, Bill's offer to lead in a closing prayer was also a sign of solidarity and support. This was a good and caring way to close the visit.

As this visit amply demonstrates, Lifestyle Relational Evangelism is *a matter of caring for others at the point of their greatest needs.* It is a sensitive approach that calls for unconditional love in building relationships, and patience in discerning needs through the guidance of the Holy Spirit in each unique situation. As a result of the way in which this visit was conducted, Bill, Mary, Jim, Cindy, and Dick have begun a new relationship — a relationship that has the promise of mutual care and support for all concerned, a relationship that already leans into the transforming power of the gospel of Jesus Christ.

LRE teams don't have a transcript to follow when they make calls in the field. Indeed, many actual calls could be much more difficult to analyze than the visit just illustrated.

Even this illustration can alert us, however, to the importance of sensitivity, caring, and relating to others as they are. Just imagine the damage that could have been done in the above situation if the team had come to Dick and Cindy with a canned presentation of the gospel. The team probably would have given the impression of an overly aggressive group of Methodists whose main purpose was to try to win converts from other denominations. Quite apart from how this would have reflected on the team, or even upon The United Methodist Church, it would have been a sad distortion of the gospel of Jesus Christ.

Follow-Up Visits

At this point we need to register boldly a very practical consideration that follows directly from the emphasis in LRE on building relationships and meeting needs: *The vast majority of visits that an LRE team makes in its ministry area will be follow-up visits,* not first-time visits. Let's put this in the form of an imperative, and remember it well:

Focus on follow-up visits more than on first-time visits.

Think about it; this is only a logical consequence of the vision and the principles that we have already discussed.

- Building a meaningful relationship with another person requires time, patience, grace, love, hope, and effort.
- Quality friendships do not just happen. They are built one day at a time over a long period of shared experience.
- Relationships that are not built with genuine sensitivity over time, relationships that are rushed according to a preconceived agenda, do not last.

Ironically, some congregations who thought they understood the spiritual vision of LRE have nearly lost their way as a result of not being clear on this practical point. The real temptation here is to keep making more and more first-time visits — perhaps trying to win instant converts — while leaving no time for the kind of follow-up visits that build long-term relationships. When this happens, a congregation can wind up treating people as a means to an end, and lose sight (in practice if not in theory) of the real vision of LRE.

From a purely statistical point of view, the mandate for instant results is, to say the least, ill-conceived. Simply put, it is very unlikely that an unchurched person will become involved in a congregation as the result of one visit. Independent research has shown that over 90 percent of persons who unite with a local church do so because they were invited by a friend or relative. Likewise, LRE congregations have discovered a number of supporting insights:

1. An average of fifteen to twenty follow-up visits is required before a new relationship reaches a meaningful level of trust and friendship.

2. An average of fifteen quality contacts with unchurched persons is required before they will respond by coming to worship or Sunday school.

3. Only one out of every fifteen unchurched persons with whom a relationship is built will decide to join the church; many of these will be on profession of faith.

Such statistics, by themselves, show the error of placing more emphasis on first-time visits than on follow-up visits. As telling as the statistics are, however, they still don't probe the full depth of the problem.

In order to identify the problem indepth, we must claim the *full range* of benefits that come from being involved in long-term ministry. For one thing, let's be clear about the benefits that come into the lives of those who visit. Every time you return with your team for a follow-up visit, you will have opportunities to learn and grow together. Your own faith will grow stronger as you see needs met, or as you learn what it means to support (and be supported by) other team members through experiences of rejection or disappointment in the field. Because you have put yourself on the line for God, you will learn what it means to draw on the strength of your Christian brothers and sisters, and to celebrate in all things.

Likewise, the commitment to long-term ministry will bring a new spirit of celebration to your congregation as a whole. One of the greatest tragedies in the local church today is our loss of celebration. We only celebrate the major victories, such as meeting the yearly budget or adding new members to the church family. These things are exciting, to be sure, but hundreds of other victories are present in the ministry of evangelism that should be shared in worship and fellowship. Think of it: Just to participate in a visit in the home of an unchurched person or family, and to find a warm reception there, is a great honor, worthy of celebration. The persons you visit have experienced the love of Christ. A positive witness has been made. The way has been prepared to share the benefits of Christ more fully, as the Spirit leads. Indeed, these are blessed events that need to be celebrated in the Body of Christ.

Why, then, do we so often miss the opportunity to celebrate these "little" things? Quite simply, we are too easily led astray by the clamor for instant results. Therefore, we must call a halt to spiritualistic headhunting. We must refuse to regard a visit with someone in our ministry area as a worthless experience unless we have had the chance to present the gospel completely. We must become sensitive to where people are, to the real problems they are facing, and to the right timing — the timing of the Spirit — in which we may have the honor and the obligation of sharing the good news of Jesus Christ. All of this will require a commitment to long-term ministry — a commitment in which the majority of LRE visits will be follow-up visits rather than first-time visits.

Now we also need to remain open to the Spirit at this point. Along with all of the benefits listed above, there will be occasions when we are called to present the gospel directly to another person. There will be times when this is the most appropriate thing to do. Some persons will come to us ready to hear the gospel; they will come with questions about their own relationships with Christ that they cannot avoid asking even if they want to. On such occasions, we have an obligation to share the gospel directly with another whose heart is being moved by the Spirit. Our witness may be crucial as a person finds the way into faith. All of this can happen, moreover, on a first visit, or a second, or a third. Let no one deny these occasions. Let all celebrate them with a full and thankful heart; but let all likewise remember that these are the exceptions, not the rule, of long-term ministry.

In this light, we might offer a provisional rule of thumb: The regular schedule of an LRE team should probably include at least three follow-up visits for every first-time visit in the ministry area. Of course, not all follow-up visits have to be of a formal nature. Indeed, as relationships grow, more and more visits will probably be of a casual, day-to-day nature. Guidelines like these are not intended to limit your vision, compassion, and goodwill; they simply offer a way to check that you and your team are really focusing on building relationships, meeting needs, and caring for the people of your ministry area in the name and Spirit of Christ.

Casual Acquaintance Visit

Now let's look at another kind of visit that applies the vision of LRE in a somewhat different way. Nearly all of us come into contact with dozens of people each week — in grocery stores, at service stations, on the street, and in other settings. The importance of long-term ministry might suggest that LRE congregations have no way of reaching out or ministering to such casual acquaintances, but this is not true. While the time frame of ministry changes, the ultimate values and goals remain the same. Imagine the following dialogue.

(John and Angie Parnell are active members of Still Branch United Methodist Church. They have just been discussing their pastor's recent sermon on reaching out to total strangers. They decide that they will give this idea a try. They walk into a local Minute Mart to pay for gas. The place is quiet and no one is there but a young woman behind the counter named Linda.)

Linda: Hello, sir, that will be $15.00 of unleaded?

John: Yes, thank you. Would you put it on this Master Card please? *(Linda waits for the credit card to be processed, while John notices a display case of caffeine tablets that are supposed to keep drivers awake.)* Can you believe people really use these things to keep themselves going?

Linda: I guess some of them need it. My trouble is getting calmed down after a day, not getting revved up.

John: Yes, I know what you mean. My life used to be like a roller coaster ride. One day I was up, and the next down. It was really hard on me and my family.

Angie: That's for sure. If he hadn't changed all that, we wouldn't be standing here together today!

Linda: That's interesting. How did you make a change like that?

John: Well, a friend of ours knew our marriage was in trouble. He really cared about us and kept telling us we needed to get into a church. He invited us all the time but we always made an excuse not to go. Then one day he told us we should at least try it for the sake of saving our marriage. So we did it just to get him off our backs.

Angie: I was not real comfortable about going to church either. I had gone some as a child, and had some bad memories about how stuffy church was. But we really wanted our marriage to get better so we decided to give it a try. It really helped us. We're closer now than ever before. *(She reaches out to put her arm in John's.)*

Linda: That's neat. I don't go to church anywhere because I use Sundays to get caught up on my housecleaning. And every other Sunday I have to work here. My husband and I have talked about sending our kids. We feel like they need to go, but we're not sure where to send them. Which church do you go to?

Angie: We go to Still Branch United Methodist on Highway 19. Do you know where it is?

Linda: Oh, yes, it's that pretty white frame church that sits in the trees?

Angie: Yes, that's it. We would love to have you and your family go with us next Sunday if you're not working. Or if you are, maybe the following Sunday? By the way, my name is Angie Parnell, and this is my husband, John.

Linda: Oh, it's nice to meet you. My name is Linda Garner. I'll talk to my husband about it and see if we can come this Sunday. Maybe it could help our family the way it did yours.

Angie: Good! Let me give you my phone number and you can call and let us know if we can meet you there this Sunday or the next. We'd be glad to have you sit with us and we could introduce you to some other people we know in the congregation. We could also help your children find the right Sunday school class if you bring them.

Linda: O.K., that sounds good. I'll check to see if we can come this coming Sunday. It's my day off and maybe we can. It was nice to meet you, and thanks for inviting us.

John and Angie made a simple trip to the gas station; they also made a significant witness for Christ and the church. Let's underscore some of the ways their visit with Linda fulfills the spiritual vision of LRE.

First, John and Angie *determined to make themselves available to share* if an opportunity presented itself. They had been given some training at church, and they were at least willing to try what they had been taught.

Second, as with all LRE visits, John *found a simple and natural way to make personal contact*. John did not insist on jumping into an explicitly religious conversation. He simply noticed the caffeine tablets and commented about their use. This gave Linda some sense of who John was and an opportunity to respond if she wanted. It was a non-threatening subject for two strangers to discuss.

Third, John was *sensitive to Linda's comment about her own needs*. To be sure, Linda did not share her needs in depth or detail, but she did express a very basic kind of openness and vulnerability. She spoke of her need to calm down at the end of the day instead of getting revved up.

Fourth, because they were sensitive to Linda, John and Angie *were able to share something of their own story as it seemed relevant to the conversation*. John's and Angie's brief account of their struggle with marriage, their reluctant trek back to church, and their newfound closeness showed their vulnerability and transparency. They were offering Linda an opportunity to take the conversation deeper, but they were not forcing her to do this. Linda was free to say nothing in response, or she might have indicated explicitly that she did not want to pursue the conversation. Instead, she expressed genuine interest.

Fifth, on the basis of Linda's interest, John and Angie *made themselves available to serve in other ways*. Angie may have sensed that Linda would be more comfortable talking woman to woman. In any event, Angie gave Linda information about the church and an invitation to attend on a specific day and time. John and Angie also made clear that they were prepared to greet Linda's family if they visited and to help them feel at home. Introductions were made at this point — formally establishing the potential for a continuing relationship. Angie conveyed a final expression of goodwill by giving her phone number to Linda.

As a result of this casual visit, a strong possibility developed that Linda and her family would reestablish some kind of meaningful contact with the church. John and Angie remained true to the first principles of LRE, but they did not turn their visit into an opportunity to corner Linda with a pushy presentation of the gospel. If John and Angie had sensed at any time that Linda was uncomfortable, they could have adjusted the depth of their own sharing while continuing to patronize the store. This would enable them to continue to relate to Linda as a friend with no strings attached.

The world is full of people like Linda. They work in Minute Marts, restaurants, offices, schools, and thousands of other places each day. If we as the church were to become seriously committed to reaching out to strangers, then the world could be dramatically changed for the good. It takes so little on our part to touch a life for Christ.

The Ministry of Correspondence

Before closing this chapter, I want to illustrate one other important element of visitation: the ministry of correspondence. Think of the last time you received an encouraging note from a personal friend — a note that had no other purpose than to express appreciation. Most of us rarely receive such notes or letters, but we remember them when we do.

LRE congregations have found that one of the most effective ways to communicate genuine care is simply to send a note expressing appreciation to those who have been visited. All that is required is for one or more team members to take a moment after the visit to write a personalized note. Depending on the nature of the visit, the note may include a well-thought-out response, or it may simply convey appreciation at meeting the people and starting a friendship. For teams who visit on Thursday nights, notes can be written during the report session, mailed the next day, and received on Saturday. Many families have come to visit the church because of receiving such a note.

A Catholic family who moved into a subdivision in our ministry area told us they were basically not church folk. We made a note of this and put them on a list for follow-up in three months because of the initial rather cool reception. In three months we went back to the home for the first follow-up and the people seemed to recognize who we were immediately. They said, "Of course, we know who you are. You're the folks who sent us the nice note after you visited. It's up there on the mantel. We've been here nearly four months now and yours is the only card anyone has sent. We love it!"

A typical note from a team may be written in the following manner:

> Dear Mr. and Mrs. Smith,
>
> It was such a joy to meet you and visit with you this evening. Your new home is lovely. We enjoyed sharing with you some of the ministries that are going on here at our church. We believe one of the most important characteristics of our congregation is Christian Love.
>
> We sincerely hope that your family can come and experience the joy of fellowship here at our church. We look forward to seeing you again in the coming days. May the Lord be with you and we are,
>
> In His Service,
>
> John Dean, Sam Rutherford, and Kimberly Clark

Even a short note such as this can serve as a significant witness to those who have been visited. Notice that it is informal and friendly. It recognizes that a new relationship has been started. It is affirming in tone, even in the way it recalls the family's home. It also expresses the team's hope to visit again. Small things, such as this note, make a great difference in the quality of care and witness that others perceive. No one can care for strangers in the community better than the local church; yet thousands of people live desperate and lonely lives in the shadow of church buildings. Unless we are willing to reach out — even in little ways — this can only be an indictment against us.

Another type of correspondence is a brief note sent to persons who have been visited over a period of time but have never responded. Again, express appreciation for previous visits, yet concern about the lack of any response. Has the person visited found another local church to attend? Is he or she no longer interested in receiving visits from your congregation? These types of letters should be used sparingly. Only those who have not responded in any way for ten to twelve months might receive one.

No matter the occasion, a personal note that expresses genuine interest and appreciation is always welcome. Indeed, writing notes is a good way to remember one of the most important of all principles of visitation:

God always uses everything we do and say for his glory.

Planting seeds is tough and wearisome work. It takes time to grow a tree and even longer for the tree to produce fruit; but if we keep in mind that God is the gardener, we will be able to faithfully work in the garden knowing that God's time is best.

Summary

Let me now summarize this very important chapter in three simple yet profound points — each addressed to you as a member of a maturing LRE team. First of all, *begin to picture your ministry area as your parish*, the place in which you will minister to the needs of others. You will be going out as a minister for Jesus Christ and his church. There is no set agenda. You have a plan, yes, but you and your team are willing to be flexible based on the needs you encounter. You are not going with a mandate to "do a presentation" of the gospel. Your mandate is to demonstrate the gospel before others.

Second, *focus on giving quality care to those you visit*. Don't be in any hurry to see how many statistics you can pile up to impress the folks back at church. You are looking for quality care to occur, and this often takes time to establish. You begin new relationships with the people in your ministry area as an intruder on their home turf. Therefore, be patient and sensitive as the love of Christ breaks down barriers of defensiveness and suspicion.

Third, *remember to keep things on a good relational level* with the persons you meet. Apart from very unusual circumstances, you cannot move directly from being strangers with another person to sharing the depths of your spiritual experience before God. The vast majority of persons need the confidence and respect of genuine friendship before they are ready or willing to discuss their spiritual journey. Begin with people where you find them. If they are outside in the yard planting flowers, then share (or learn) about flowers. If they are walking a dog, then show some interest in their pet.

In all, remember to look to the New Testament and to how Jesus reached out to persons where they were and related to them at the point of their greatest needs. He related to people in this way in order to reach them for the kingdom of God. That is our calling, too. Press on; move out beyond the walls with Christ.

❖ 7. Administering the Movement

The effectiveness of your LRE ministry will depend in large measure on how well you keep track of the ongoing results of long-term visitation. In a word, it will depend on your skill in the art of *administration*. Think about it: If your congregation becomes fully engaged in LRE, you will have a number of visitation teams going out each week to conduct a variety of first-time and follow-up visits. Over a period of months, you will have contacted dozens if not hundreds of individuals and families. Some of these people will have responded eagerly to your offer of friendship and support. Others will affirm your efforts, but will want you to understand that they are already actively involved in another congregation. A few others may react to your visit and request that visitation teams from the church not return. How will you keep track of so many different needs and responses? How will you insure that teams remember all of this information in order to minister effectively? These are questions that point to the importance of the ministry of administration.

An effective ministry of administration has several benefits. First, it enables and equips LRE teams to give quality care to the people of their ministry areas. As teams follow up on earlier visits, they will have their own notes to remind them of the people they have met — their names, questions, interests, and the needs that may have been expressed. Teams will also have a record of other interactions or responses that other members of the congregation may have initiated. Effective administration facilitates team response and congregational involvement without losing track of earlier experiences that are so vital in the development of ongoing relationships.

The ministry of administration is also an area in which some members of the congregation will find a place to exercise their personal spiritual gifts. In Acts 6 we find a record of how the early church called a group of special leaders to oversee the distribution of services to those with needs in the community. Stephen and six others who were "full of faith" and "full of the Spirit and of wisdom" were appointed to watch over the weekly distribution of food, especially to widows. Likewise, the apostle Paul made several lists of spiritual gifts in which he affirmed the importance of skills that entail administration (see Romans 12:6-8; 1 Corinthians 12:4-10, 27-28; and Ephesians 4:11-16). Administration is a special gift. Not everyone is called to it; not everyone can do it effectively. For those who are called and gifted, this is a wonderful way to be involved in the ministry of LRE.

So what are the components of administration? How is administrative information gathered and distributed? Who handles this information and for what purposes? Even in the brief descriptions already given we can see the basic outline: Teams gather information while they visit. They share appropriate information with others in the LRE ministry (and in the congregation) in order to broaden the base for responding to needs. Information is then filed in a central office where administrative leaders can make sure that it will be reactivated as new teams go out or as follow-up visits are made. All of this requires a set of basic forms for recording information and a filing system for keeping track of the information as it develops. Let's look at each of these components in more detail.

The Initial Visit Form

The first contact that your LRE ministry has with people will often come as the result of a first-time visit. In the last two chapters we described some of the dynamics of this kind of visit. As the team leader and the support person engage in conversation, the team recorder gathers basic information on the "Initial Visit Form" (see sample on page 61). As mentioned before, this can be done in an open and polite manner. The information requested on the form does not reach beyond what is commonly shared in polite conversation. If those being visited ask about the form, show it to them and explain its purpose: to get to know them better and to consider how your congregation may be of service. All team members should periodically study the form in order to stay familiar with the kinds of questions that are appropriate for an initial visit.

Since we have already described the nature of initial visits in the last two chapters, we needn't spend a great deal of time on that here. There is, however, one question on the Initial Visit Form that deserves further comment. This has to do with whether or not those visited are currently active in another local church.

The question about church involvement can be pivotal in the conduct of a first visit. If those visited are active in another congregation, the first visit still has value; but a follow-up visit is not usually appropriate. The members of two congregations have met each other. If they have been open, they may have learned something of what the other is doing in ministry. Depending on the nature of the visit, moreover, relationships may or may not develop in new directions. Congregations collaborate in ministry all the time, but LRE teams are *not* out to take people away from other congregations.

We must be crystal clear on this point: *We are not out to proselyte active members of another local church.* If those visited are active in another local church, we should celebrate this with them on the spot. We can even take this one step further by asking them to call on a group in their congregation to lift our visitation ministry in prayer. This can be a marvelous witness to our unity in faith and to our seriousness about true evangelism. When we move in this way to support one another in ministry, the surrounding community will also come to know that our congregations are committed to ministry, not institutional survival.

Someone might want to press the issue at this point: "Jim, this is all fine if you are talking about people who are members of another United Methodist congregation, but what if they belong to another denomination?" The answer is basically the same. In the ministry of Lifestyle Relational Evangelism we are not called to function as denominational sales representatives. We seek to minimize denominational differences, and we are not out to gather members away from other denominations. Even when the topic of denominational loyalties comes up in the context of a visit, we seek to move to other areas of commonality. We are proud to be United Methodists and we realize that there are some major differences between our communion and others; but the Body of Christ also has a universal character that transcends all our differences and reminds us of what we hold in common.*

---

* This response applies to mainstream denominations — for example, Baptist, Presbyterian, Catholic, Church of Christ, etc. Readers are urged, however, to study critically the teachings and practices of other groups, sects, or cults such as Jehovah's Witnesses, and the Church of Jesus Christ of Latter Day Saints, commonly known as Mormons. The latter are both extremely diligent in their efforts, and can appear to be sincere and warm in personality; but they depart in dangerous ways from the essential teachings of classical, biblical Christianity.

INITIAL VISIT FORM

Date: ___/___/___ Team members: _____

Family name: _____

Address: _____

City: _____ Zip code: _____

Is this family **presently active in a local church**?   Yes _____   No _____

Church background: _____

Family Names and Information

Head of household: _____

Spouse: _____

Child #1: _____

Child #2: _____

Child #3: _____

Child #4: _____

Others in home: _____

_____

Present needs: _____

_____

Head of household place of employment: _____

Spouse's employment: _____

Hobbies, interests, etc.: _____

Telephone nos.: Home: _____ Work: _____

Follow-up visit to be made?   Yes _____   No _____   If yes, when? ___/___/___

Visitation Zone: _____

Even with this conciliatory attitude in mind, LRE teams will encounter some people who feel the need to stress denominational differences. In this regard, teams have learned to diffuse arguments in several ways. A team might stress, for example, that its primary purpose is simply to share the love of Jesus Christ and to build caring relationships with those being visited. On the other hand, the team might be able to disarm the debate by inserting an all-too-true bit of humor: "The name of the denomination on the sign out front is no guarantee of the quality of caring on the inside." This is true whether one is talking about one's own denomination or another. Even denominational loyalists will usually be able to acknowledge the truth of this statement.

Now let's press this one step further. What if the person being visited *was* affiliated with another denomination *in the past*, but is *not currently active* in any congregation? As we saw in the last chapter, Dick Reeves insisted on his Baptist affiliation though he and his wife Cindy were not active in a Baptist congregation or in any other. Was Dick really committed to his Baptist roots though temporarily out of touch? Or was his Baptist background simply a convenient way to keep the team at arm's length? These are questions the visiting team was not really in a position to answer during the first visit. They needed to get to know Dick and Cindy better in order to have discernment. Eventually, they might be instrumental in helping the Reeves reclaim their heritage in a specific Baptist congregation; or Dick and Cindy might decide, like Mary and her husband, that they wanted to join the fellowship of Christians at First United Methodist Church in Rockledge. In any event, the team learned enough during the first visit to feel that they could invite the Reeveses to worship and Sunday school without undermining the ministry of another congregation or denomination.

All of this suggests an important principle that should be observed in relating to *inactive* persons. Distinguish between church membership and active involvement in a congregation. LRE teams have learned *not* to ask simply if someone is a "member" of a church. Many people are members somewhere, but like Dick and Cindy they are not actively involved. This is why the Initial Visit Form asks not only about church background but also about *present activity*. In situations such as that of the Reeves family, LRE teams should be open to the possibility of ministry regardless of denominational background. In essence, LRE teams will want to communicate the following message:

Our congregation gladly welcomes ALL persons.

Lifestyle Relational Evangelism is a proactive ministry, but it is not offensive. With its roots in The United Methodist Church, LRE springs from a tradition that embraces the diverse strengths and emphases of world Christianity. This proactive posture is always tempered, moreover, by Christian love and sensitivity to the needs of others. Evangelism programs that are offensive are a dime-a-dozen. Sensitivity to the needs of others and genuine Christian love are all too often in short supply. Our primary and ultimate objective — whether we are on a first-time visit or a follow-up visit — is to love, meet needs, and build relationships for the kingdom. This, after all, was the ministry plan of Christ.

The Follow-Up Visit Form

Initial visits are only the beginning of the process of relationship building. Even more crucial is the follow-up aspect of this ministry. One of the most crucial elements of effective follow-up visits, moreover, is the recollection of accurate information from previous visits; but how can anyone remember so much information?

One of the first things to recognize about follow-up visits is that they may be numerous and the same team members may not be present at each visit. Though LRE stresses the importance of long-term involvement of each team in its ministry area, we also need to be realistic. Team members cannot always remember the details of earlier visits. Likewise, the composition of a team may change for some reason — for example, when the needs of one's own family, or other commitments, call a team member away. Whatever the reason, teams need a way of refreshing their own memories about the details of earlier visits as they prepare to go out on follow-up visits.

In this light, LRE congregations have developed a Follow-Up Visit Form (see page 64). This form is used to record information from each follow-up visit in order to prepare for future visits. The entire history of visitation with each household can be summarized on follow-up forms, and these forms can be kept in a file folder along with the Initial Visit Form for each household. Then, before making additional visits, team members can review the file to refresh their memories concerning names, interests, and needs as shared previously.

Using the information available in the file, follow-up visits should focus on several issues. For instance, team members should be prepared to *call persons by name*. This is simply part of building a good relationship. Friends call each other by name. Greeted in this way, those visited will soon come to learn the names of team members as well. Before long, all will feel more like friends than strangers.

Likewise, follow-up visits should focus on the *needs of persons being visited*. Those visited may hint at any time or share openly about their interests and needs. Are they planting a new garden? Have they just purchased a new television? Is a child leaving for college? Has a relative become ill? All of these and many other interests and concerns can become a topic of conversation. Teams should give people every opportunity to talk about their families, needs, interests, and just how they are doing. If team members are sensitive, they can establish a sense of common interest and concern. Those visited will notice when someone outside their household is close enough to ask about something meaningful to them. Such care is all too rare in our society.

Another important consideration has to do with how *frequently* a team should follow up with an individual or a family. Notice that the Initial Visit Form (page 61) includes a line for recommending a specific date for the first follow-up visit. Likewise, the Follow-Up Visit Form includes lines for recommended dates of subsequent visits. On what basis, however, do teams make these recommendations?

In most cases, there is no way to predict the best schedule for follow-up. Some families will look forward to each visit, and relationships will deepen at a rapid pace. Others will seem noncommittal about receiving another visit. Teams should not be discouraged by this attitude. Those visited may be having a bad day or they may be struggling with an issue that has nothing to do with the team or its visit. If the person you are following up does not want to be visited again, this too will usually become apparent. Through it all, teams must use common sense on a case-by-case basis. Trust your instincts, but don' t give up too easily.

A somewhat different question has to do with how *long* a team should continue to visit with a particular person or family. Perhaps the best answer to this is simply to say that we will continue to reach out to someone as long as there is hope of building a relationship.

FOLLOW-UP VISIT FORM

Family name: _____

Date of initial visit: ___/___/___

Team members at initial visit: _____

❖ ❖ ❖

FOLLOW-UP #1   Date: ___/___/___

Team members: _____

Current needs/other: _____

_____

Follow-up recommended on ___/___/___

❖ ❖ ❖

FOLLOW-UP #2   Date: ___/___/___

Team members: _____

Current needs/other: _____

_____

Follow-up recommended on ___/___/___

❖ ❖ ❖

FOLLOW-UP #3   Date: ___/___/___

Team members: _____

Current needs/other: _____

_____

Follow-up recommended on ___/___/___

Some of the most vital Christians in congregations today are persons who received years of visitation before they ever entered a church building. Moreover, something can be said for people who decide to join a congregation only after establishing a relationship of genuine respect and care. Most of these persons will make a change not only of mind, but also of heart and *lifestyle*; such is their integrity.

Nevertheless, persons do at times make it clear that they want nothing more to do with the church. When this happens, we must press on in the love of Christ to other individuals and families. Even as you read this, there are literally thousands of people who need the love of Christ made real in their lives by the gentle care of Christ's followers. Take just a moment now to repeat this statement to yourself out loud:

Jesus wants to use me to reach others.

Motivated by the love of Christ, this affirmation will resonate in our hearts. Reflect on this, then make a commitment to live it with his help.

The Report Session Form

Another responsibility of the ministry of administration is to conduct a report session for the visitation teams after they return to the church building. The benefits of such a session are several.

First, this is an opportunity for teams to share information and to celebrate victories both large and small. During the report session, one person on each team is asked to give a report of the team's experiences. The Report Session Form (see page 66) serves as a general guideline for the person making this verbal report to the rest of the group. This is an important time, as everyone gets to hear the names of new persons who have been contacted, to pray for the relationships that are being formed, and to give thanks for the needs that are being met.

Likewise, the information shared in the report session also broadens the ability of the congregation to respond to those visited. On Sunday morning, if one of those visited should attend Sunday school or worship, the new name will be recognized by all in the visitation ministry. The Report Session Form also includes a space for teams to indicate special needs to pastoral staff. In short, the report session process insures that those visited will receive as broad a base of support in the congregation as possible.

Put yourself in the picture. Your team has gone into a home and discovered that a relative of the family being visited is in the local hospital. During the visit, your team leader prays for this need, but this is only the beginning of your total response. Your team will record this need and share it at the report session so others can be praying as well. Then the need can be conveyed in appropriate ways to prayer and sharing groups in the congregation. You or someone else on your team will send an encouraging note to the family, thanking them for the opportunity to meet them, and letting them know of ways your congregation would like to offer support (prayer, food, hospital visitation). In all, this family will know that you and your congregation have taken their need to heart. This is the church in action.

Another benefit of the report session is raw data about the community. When Report Session Forms are filled in accurately and completely, administrative leaders can compile a variety of statistical data that will be useful in future ministry. For example, at the close of

REPORT SESSION FORM

Date of this report: ____/____/____

Team leader: _____

Team members: _____

Initial visits attempted on this trip: _____

Initial visits completed on this trip: _____

Follow-up calls attempted on this trip: _____

Follow-up calls completed on this trip: _____

Prayer needs to be sent to Prayer Committee:

1) _____

2) _____

3) _____

4) _____

Greatest blessing of this trip: _____

_____

_____

Thank you notes written and turned into administrators for mailing: Yes _____ No _____

Any referrals to the pastoral staff needed from visits made?   Yes _____ No _____

If yes, to whom? _____

_____

each evening of visitation, with Report Session Forms in hand, administrators can quickly total the number of initial and follow-up visits made on that night. This information can be studied by those in leadership in order to look for trends in the responses of various ministry areas or at different times of year.

The Team Leader's Kit

As we have seen, the ministry of administration involves a number of forms and steps. Team leaders, team members, and administrators must work in harmony. In order to insure that all the needed information is gathered and recorded at the appropriate time, LRE congregations have discovered the wisdom of creating a kit for each team leader. As teams prepare to go into their ministry areas, each team leader should check his or her kit to be sure that the team has all the materials it will need. These materials can be carried in briefcases, folders, or any other kind of bag or container. In any case, they need to be large enough to hold all materials and handy enough to keep the materials ready for use. Some teams like to carry the whole kit with them on each visit. Other teams prefer to leave the bulk of the kit in the car, carrying only a small clipboard and the forms necessary for the visit at hand. Here is a suggested list of supplies to be included in each team leader's kit.

1. Professionally printed brochures about the congregation
2. Maps of the area showing how to get to the church building
3. Initial Visit Forms
4. Follow-Up Visit Forms
5. Report Session Forms
6. A small clipboard (6" x 9") for the team reporter to use as a portable writing table
7. Business cards from the senior pastor and other staff persons who provide pastoral care
8. A list and description of all Sunday school classes
9. Current copies of the congregation's most recent newsletter
10. Additional information about specific ministries of the local church, such as kindergarten, child-care, Bible school, etc.
11. Door hangers to be left on doorknobs
12. Two copies of a modern translation of the New Testament to be given away to persons who do not own a Bible (an astonishing number)
13. Copies of *An Invitation from Your United Methodist Friends* tract (Discipleship Resources)
14. Copies of *Why Not Make Your Church Home Here?* tract (Discipleship Resources)

Filing Systems

Just as team leaders need kits to keep their materials organized, so administrators need a filing system to keep information organized and available. Filing systems for your LRE ministry can be as basic as a box of 3" x 5" index cards, or as sophisticated as a computer system with a full scale database program. (I recommend *Act! The Best Selling Contact Manager*, for Windows and DOS. Contact Software Int., Inc., 699 Hertel Avenue, Buffalo, NY 14207.) The key to any filing system, however, is efficiency, not looks or equipment.

Filing systems are constantly changing. The secret is to use them and to improve them as time marches on.

Regardless of filing system variables, LRE congregations have found that certain pieces of equipment and related processes are very helpful. You will want to be sure that you can account in some way for each of the following three items:

1. An office-size filing cabinet with two standard letter-size filing drawers (more as your ministry grows)
2. A file folder for each household that has been visited — your permanent record of all information gathered from visits to the household which remains active as long as follow-up visits are still being made
3. A cross-referencing system that allows administrators to classify and retrieve information in any one of three ways: alphabetical listing of households by family name, distribution of households according to ministry areas, and frequency of visits made in chronological order

The importance of being able to retrieve files in chronological order has to do with keeping track of follow up visits in a timely manner. How will you keep track of whom to follow up and when? The best approach is to create groups of "dated" files according to the dates recommended by teams for next visits. These groupings contain the files of all families who are to be followed up within a certain period of time. Then, when the date for follow-up arrives, a specific group of files can simply be pulled and made available to the teams who are going out to visit.

Let's look at an example. The Smith family was initially visited on 1/14/95. The team leader suggested at that time that the Smiths should be visited next on 2/11/95. Between 1/14 and 2/11 the team will make many other visits. How will they remember to retrieve the Smiths' file? On the night of 1/14 an administrator will place the Smiths' file in a group folder labeled "for follow-up on 2/11." Then, when the evening of 2/11 arrives, the Smiths' file will reemerge along with others that need follow-up on that night. The credibility of visitation teams is directly related to their faithfulness in following up on those previously visited. An effective filing system is an essential component in this process.

The ministry of administration may sometimes seem to be an impersonal task. In reality, it is one of the most personal things we do in the ministry of Lifestyle Relational Evangelism. It is the edge that insures our caring is quality and consistent. It gives us accountability and keeps us responsible to the needs we encounter. Those who bring in the harvest have a joyful task, yet those who break ground and plant seeds are even more to be honored. The latter know what it is to hope against hope that something will happen through faith. When there was yet nothing to see but a vision, they acted in faith and the end result is the joy of the harvest. Let us learn to rejoice as much in the discipline of planting as in the beauty of harvest. With God's help, and in God's own time, one will lead to the other.

❖ 8. Following the Spirit

Lifestyle Relational Evangelism depends above all on following the Holy Spirit. Only by following the Spirit do we find energy, insight, and love sufficient to the task. Following the Spirit does not mean, however, that we will not plan — make maps, organize teams, record information, keep files, and all of the other detailed work that we have discussed. Indeed, we might try to follow the Spirit without planning, and we might try to plan without following the Spirit; but the way of excellence is to plan *and* to follow the Holy Spirit. In this way our plans will open to the Spirit's promptings and to the Spirit's way of evaluating results.

Divine Appointments

LRE congregations have learned through experience not to underestimate the ability of the Holy Spirit to lead visitation teams into specific ministry situations. Indeed, we have come to refer to this kind of specific leading by means of a special phrase: *divine appointment*. When we risk ourselves for Jesus Christ, divine appointments occur, but what do we really mean by divine appointments?

To begin with, let's be clear: We are not speaking of any kind of "hocus-pocus theology" in which secret phenomena occur. Divine appointments are not strange events; nor do they require mysterious perceptive powers. Rather, a divine appointment is simply a situation in which we are led by the Holy Spirit to discern where we need to be in ministry. Each divine appointment represents an opportunity for ministry to occur. There are many examples of divine appointments in the Bible. One of the best known accounts concerns a disciple of Jesus named Philip (Acts 8:26-40):

> *Then an angel of the Lord said to Philip, "Get up and go toward the south to the road that goes down from Jerusalem to Gaza." (This is a wilderness road.) So he got up and went. Now there was an Ethiopian eunuch, a court official of the Candace, queen of the Ethiopians, in charge of her entire treasury. He had come to Jerusalem to worship and was returning home; seated in his chariot, he was reading the prophet Isaiah. Then the Spirit said to Philip, "Go over to his chariot and join it." So Philip ran up to it and heard him reading the prophet Isaiah. He asked, "Do you understand what you are reading?" He replied, "How can I, unless someone guides me?" And he invited Philip to get in and sit beside him. Now the passage of the scripture that he was reading was this:*
>
>> *"Like a sheep he was led to the slaughter, and like a lamb silent before its shearer, so he does not open his mouth. In his humiliation justice was denied him. Who can describe his generation? For his life is taken away from the earth."*
>
> *The eunuch asked Philip, "About whom, may I ask, does the prophet say this, about himself or about someone else?" Then Philip began to speak, and starting with this*

scripture, he proclaimed to him the good news about Jesus. As they were going along the road, they came to some water; and the eunuch said, "Look, here is water! What is to prevent me from being baptized?" He commanded the chariot to stop, and both of them, Philip and the eunuch, went down into the water, and Philip baptized him. When they came up out of the water, the Spirit of the Lord snatched Philip away; the eunuch saw him no more, and went on his way rejoicing. But Philip found himself at Azotus, and as he was passing through the region, he proclaimed the good news to all the towns until he came to Caesarea.

Notice in this account how Philip followed the leading of the Spirit without resistance. He might have objected that the road to which he felt led was not a good choice; it was a desert road. He might have worried that he should not bother someone so important as the Ethiopian official; Philip could have been mistaken for a robber or a troublemaker and put to death. Instead, Philip listened and followed the direction of the Spirit's leading. The Lord did not have to tell him many times or in many ways. Philip knew he was trusting the Spirit. He did not have to worry about what he would say or how things would turn out.

Someone might look at this account and object: "Well, that was O.K. for Philip; he was a disciple, and everything turned out well for him." We should remember, however, that Philip did not know at the beginning how things would turn out. So what does this story mean for us today? When is the last time an angel of the Lord appeared and told us to go anywhere? Could this happen to us today? The answer to that question is an unequivocal yes! Let me illustrate from personal experience.

As LRE began to grow at County Line United Methodist Church, other congregations began to hear of what was happening. We were asked at the end of our first year in the ministry to submit several 35mm slides which would be shared at annual conference the next June. One specific request was for us to include a slide showing some of our own people helping a family move into a new home with a moving van in the yard. This request seemed simple enough. We had helped people in this situation before. A slide such as this would illustrate how exciting and simple it can be to reach out to people at the point of their most immediate needs; but, as time passed, the request became more and more difficult to fulfill. It seemed that moving vans suddenly became scarce in our community, with only two weeks until the deadline for these slides to be submitted.

I was not worried though. I had called several major moving companies in northwest Atlanta and Cobb County and asked them to call me if a truck was heading toward our area. All of them seemed cooperative enough and assured me they would call when a truck was scheduled to come in our direction. Days passed with no calls. Now there was less than one week until the deadline.

The frequency of my prayers increased regarding this need. I knew that God had blessed our ministry, and I believed that the Spirit wanted to use us in every way possible to help other congregations catch the vision. But as the days passed, I began to wonder if these special slides would ever be made. I put my camera equipment in my car each day and had several of our laity "on standby" who would come to help and would appear in the pictures if I called them on short notice.

Monday was the deadline. It was Friday morning now. I had spent several hours that week driving through housing developments hoping a moving van would suddenly appear.

All team leaders were alerted to also scour their ministry areas, but we could not locate a moving van anywhere. None were found, even with all our concerted efforts and prayers.

That morning I was leaving West Cobb County to take my youngest son, Jonathan, to kindergarten at First United Methodist Church in Marietta. I was tense and was beginning to accept the possibility that we would not be able to line up pictures with a moving van. I dropped Jonathan off and, as I drove across the parking lot, I felt the need to stop and pray. I did. I knew that the pictures themselves were not the important thing. Reaching out to people in need and helping other congregations to catch the vision of this kind of ministry — those were the goals. So with the engine running and the radio on, I prayed, "Lord, I know that all things are possible with you. I've done all I know to do about these slides. So I'll just sit here and listen for your guidance."

As my eyes opened I glanced across the hood of the car toward the intersection of Whitlock Avenue and Powder Springs Street. Just as I put my car in gear, I saw a big, bright blue moving van come through the intersection. I felt warm all over. Then my mind said to me, "Hollis, this is ridiculous. You are really getting a little fanatical!" I said out loud, "We'll see. Why not believe it?"

I fell in behind the huge tractor-trailer going west on Whitlock past McDonald's. I read the tags on the truck — Alabama plates. Again I thought, "This is dumb. You know prayers don't get answered this way." Suddenly, I looked down and noticed my gas gauge was on "Empty." It was one of those gauges where empty really means empty! The gas stations were now behind me, we were out of town, and the truck was speeding up.

Then I sensed a voice in my thoughts, "The van is about to pull over up here. Get ready to put on your brakes and pull over right behind it. You get out and talk to the driver." I thought to myself that I must have suddenly become eligible for mental illness insurance funds. There was nowhere on this road for a vehicle of that size to pull off — no stations or other stores within five miles of us. To my amazement, however, the right rear blinker of the trailer came on, indicating that the van was about to pull off on the shoulder. There was a small gravel area just to the right where a construction site had been started. I could hardly believe this was happening. I pulled off behind it, reaching for my handkerchief to wipe the tears from my face.

I really didn't know what I would say as I got out of my car and approached the cab of the Kenworth rig. I was nearly speechless. Then a large man opened the door of the cab and jumped out right in front of me. He looked very surprised to see me and I was certainly shocked to see him!

He said, "Hello there, mister. Where in the world did you come from?"

I said, "Well, it's a long story." Before I could get another word out of my mouth he spoke again.

"Well, I'm glad to see you. We're lost. We're looking for West Hampton subdivision. Do you know where it is?"

"Come on, I'll lead you there," I said, knowing exactly where the entrance of the subdivision was.

So there I was, driving down Highway 120, below empty on the gas gauge, with a massive van behind me. My stomach was full of butterflies, and all I could say was, "Lord, it's up to you. This is completely out of my hands now."

West Hampton is a development of $300,000 homes located in the Due West community.

It was one subdivision in West Cobb I had refused to go into because it was located less than one mile from Due West United Methodist Church, one of our sister churches. As a result, I didn't know the layout of streets and houses.

I turned on my blinker and turned in at the development entrance. I felt that if I just continued on this main road, then the street I was looking for would surely be close. I crept along, looking everywhere for the street. Several street signs went by. The van was all I could see and hear behind me. Then the street sign appeared on the right. I breathed a sigh of relief.

As we turned onto the deadend street, I was suddenly staring at nearly twenty-five new homes and a street filled with workers, cars, and trucks. How would I know which house? Then I saw a man standing near the end of a driveway and I knew that was the one. We waved at each other. The movers motioned to me that they were going to turn around and tapped the air horn as my signal. I got out of the car and walked over to the man in the driveway.

He said hello. Then it hit me. What was I going to say to him? The van was turning around in the cul-de-sac as I began to explain.

"Oh, good morning," he said. "I bet you're a representative from the moving company. We have some things all ready inside. Come on in and I'll show you where to start."

We went in. He introduced me by name to his wife who was very friendly also. They asked me if I had papers. I said, "Well, I have something you need to know. I'm a United Methodist pastor from one of the local churches here. (He looked at me with utter suspicion.) It's really hard to explain, but I found this moving van on the side of the road and gave the driver directions to your house." About that time one of the movers walked in the open door. The man looked at him and then back at me.

To the mover he said, "Is this guy for real? He says he's a Methodist pastor who found you lost on the road. Is that true?"

The mover smiled and said, "Yes, sir. That's just what happened, but I don't know where he came from yet! We never would have found this place without him."

After the movers began to unload, the owner of the home began to thank me. I shared with him the rest of the story and he told me his family had moved here from North Carolina. He said he would be glad for me to bring some folks over to help them, so we got the pictures for the slides.

As we sat down together, his wife seemed very moved by all that had taken place. She said to me, "It's really strange. As we were driving over here on the interstate, we were discussing the need to find a local United Methodist church. But I had no idea that it would be like this. We want to come visit your congregation. It has to be a wonderful place!" They came to worship at County Line.

Scripture and Prayer

Now some may say that this was all a coincidence, but they have never experienced a divine appointment. The best news is that any Christian can have divine appointments. Such experiences can become a normal part of daily life if we are open to the leading of the Holy Spirit. The question can be meaningfully asked, however, "How do we know if we are being led by the Spirit? Isn't it possible to be misled by our own intentions, by the power of suggestion, or, worse yet, by the power of evil?"

These are important questions, and we must address them here, even if only briefly. When we talk about divine appointments, we are talking about how God intervenes in our lives in order to direct us to intervene in the lives of others. This is serious business. We must be careful at this point and realize that we are speaking about the spiritual realm. Scripture warns us to test the spirits and to discern whether or not they are of God. Once again, however, this does not require any kind of strange hocus-pocus theology, for we have also been given some very down-to-earth tools to guide and inform our discernment.

The first tool we have been given to guide us in following the Holy Spirit is scripture. The Bible is God's timeless message to a world that is ever-changing. It is our answer to the needs of this life and our compass to the world to come. By immersing ourselves in scripture on a regular basis, moreover, we open our minds and hearts to the leading of the Spirit. The scripture itself proclaims that the Spirit and the Word agree (1 John 5:7). Indeed, the primary way to test the spiritual character of an action or a decision is to ask whether or not it reflects the character of Christ as witnessed in scripture (John 16:13-15).

In this light, the Holy Spirit uses scripture to keep our minds and hearts focused on the things that really matter. We need to recover the excitement and expectation of the first disciples — witnessed again and again in scripture — that the Spirit really can lead us in the discovery and discernment of ministry. At the same time, the important thing is not *how* the Spirit speaks, but *who* the Spirit is — the Spirit of Christ — and *what* the Spirit will lead us to do in serving others in the name of Christ. If we pray for the guidance of the Holy Spirit as we read and study the Bible, we will find that the Lord will begin to lead us in powerful ways.

Thus, prayer is the second tool God has given to help us follow the Holy Spirit. As we tune our hearts to the Spirit of Christ in each situation, we will experience the promptings and nudgings of the Spirit concerning which way to go and what to do. The living, risen Christ wants to lead us in this way. Nevertheless, serious prayer is foreign to many in the churches today — both lay and clergy.

What is missing more than anything else in the modern practice of prayer is the ability to listen. Somewhere along the line we seem to have learned that prayer is mainly talking to God. Perhaps talkative prayer is a result of living in an activist culture where success is usually measured more by what we do (and how quickly) than by who we are. The greatest spiritual leaders throughout the history of the church have known otherwise. It is often only when we calm ourselves that we begin to listen for the voice of God (1 Kings 19:12; Psalm 46:10). Meaningful evangelism is based on a firm foundation of prayer — a capacity to listen for the Spirit's leading every moment of every day. This is the lifestyle Christ wants for us, and it is available to every Christian. Let me illustrate just how simple and down-to-earth this way of following the Spirit really is.

Soon after I came to County Line United Methodist Church as pastor, I was introduced to Hinton Brown — a man who had a reputation for being one of the most down-to-earth, no-nonsense members of the congregation. Some even regarded Hinton as a pessimist. I remember the first few times I was around Hinton. He was exactly as he had been described to me. Hinton knew how to take the opposing point to view. If you said red, he said blue. If you said good, he would insist on bad. He was quite fearless and relentless in his opinions.

Hinton was also a man who believed in the old school of marriage and family obligations. He was used to certain comforts and expectations in daily life. He knew when certain times of day came around that meals would take place. Marjorie, his wife, truly loved him. She wanted only the best for him and was quite agreeable about providing Hinton with the comforts he expected; but then something changed. Marjorie decided she wanted to participate in the ministry of LRE. She wanted to be involved in visitation ministry each Thursday night.

This was not very popular with Hinton. It meant that his supper schedule would be hampered. It also meant he would be at home alone on Thursday nights. That was O.K. for a time, but then Hinton decided he needed to come down to the church building and take a closer look at what went on at visitation — perhaps to find some problem that no one else had noticed. He came. I remember his attitude at first was along the lines that he was "just there to observe." Nevertheless, he continued to show up.

One Thursday evening I asked Hinton to go with me on my team. I had no other partners for that evening, so it would be just the two of us. To everyone's amazement, he agreed. This was one of the finest things that had ever happened to the visitation ministry. If Hinton would go, anyone would go.

Over the next two years, Hinton and I grew as close as family. I saw a real change in his attitude and spirit as the months went by. He truly cared for others and came to a point where he would not miss visitation for anything. More and more people in and out of our congregation were inspired by Hinton's new ministry involvement.

As we grew closer, we talked more and more about the whole concept of divine appointments, and following the Spirit. Hinton had heard many people talk about these holy encounters, but he felt, at that time, that he had never been directly involved in one himself.

One Thursday night we were out making some follow-up calls to several families that were on the schedule for that week. We did not find anyone at home and we were on our way back to the church building. We had stopped at a major intersection at Highway 41, just outside of Acworth, Georgia. Hinton asked me, "Just how do you know when you have one of these leadings from the Holy Spirit? I mean, how can you really know for sure?"

"Just pray hard, Hinton. Listen closely and trust in what you hear in your thoughts," I offered. I suggested that we take a minute right then to lift our hearts in prayer as we sat at this notoriously long traffic light. We did. As I opened my eyes I asked him a question.

"Well, Hinton, did anyone come to mind?"

"Yes. Do you remember Teresa? She's the one that lives over in the Meadows Subdivision."

"But, Hinton, that's way over in Paulding County! Do you know how long it'll take to get there from here?"

"Look, Mr. Hollis, you just asked me to tell you who came to mind and I did! What's your problem?"

"O.K., Hinton. If that's the message you got, then we're on our way, brother." We turned west and drove hard for about twenty minutes to the subdivision. As we entered the yard, we noticed one car in the driveway. We got out and walked up to the front door of the house. I told Hinton to knock on the door. This was his call. He did, and the door pushed open. A little girl just about six years old was standing in the hallway as the door swung open. Our eyes went down the hallway into the kitchen where we saw the girl's mother sitting on top of the kitchen counter. She was sobbing loudly and visibly shaken. One outstretched hand was full of tranquilizers and the other held a bottle.

Looking at us she said, "Don't bother me. I'm going to end it all right here. My husband came home today and told me he didn't love me anymore. He said he was getting his things and I would never see him again. He did. He's gone and I can't go on like this."

We got the pills. We helped her find help. She began to see a counselor. She eventually got a divorce, but her life was saved and she was happily remarried later on.

Hinton was never the same after that night. He was a new light for Christ. God had placed directions in Hinton's mind and his faithfulness had touched a life in a profound way. As Hinton shared his story with others after that night, he had a new light in his eyes. Pessimism was gone and joy flowed like a river. Holy encounters are like that. They touch everyone involved in profound ways, and the results are permanent.

There are people like that young woman and her daughter around every local church in America. Even as you read this book, somewhere near your congregation is a little girl wishing she knew how to make the hurting stop; or a small boy who would give anything to have some peace in his family. Marriage problems, drug abuse, domestic violence, child abuse, and countless other situations fueled by darkness surround our local churches. Who will reach out to those in pain today? The government will not. The community at large will not. Even friends avoid this kind of situation because of limited resources and knowledge. Who has the power and the resources to deal with life in this way?

The One who ordered the wind and sea to be still has the power. He holds the resources and the answers. We are his hands and feet, his eyes and ears in the world. He calls the church to go and care. The message is clear to us: Jesus will use us in our own communities to touch and transform lives if we will be faithful in going. This is what following the Spirit is all about.

The Power of Presence

Following the Spirit of Christ in this way will produce amazing results, but it will also teach you to look at results in an entirely new way. In essence, you will learn to trust that the Holy Spirit always takes care of results. Your task is not to get results, but simply to be faithful. What a joy it is for this to take place in a Christian's life! As you go out into the field of need in this way, moreover, you will learn not to evaluate visits according to a standard of immediate results — whether or not you are well received, for example, or whether or not someone decides to join your congregation. By contrast, the true value of your visitation will only come over the long haul, as you develop a *power of presence* in your ministry area.

Think about what it will mean to trust the Spirit in this way on an evening of visitation such as the following: The first household you visit is already involved in another congregation. At the second house, the people make it clear that they are not interested in a visit with anyone from a church. The couple who live in the third house are friendly, but they have guests and can't stop to visit right now. At the fourth and final home on your schedule for the evening, you meet a family who says that they have been searching for a church home. They welcome you in for a visit. How will the Holy Spirit lead you to evaluate an evening of visits like these?

In every case, the Spirit of Christ will give you ways of seeing, caring, and hoping, that reach beyond the standard of immediate results. When you meet people who are members of another congregation, the Spirit will show you an opportunity to pray and support one another in mutual ministry. When you encounter someone who is totally disenchanted with the church, the Spirit will give you respect for his or her freedom, and hope that someday in the future you may have opportunity to care again and, perhaps, to understand the sources of such reaction. Should your team visit at that house ever again? Perhaps not if you are convinced that this could only bring offense. But this too is something that you and your team can commit to prayer.

When you find a home where the people cannot receive you for a visit right then, you will be ready to offer to return at another time and even to set a date for the following week if that is possible. Since you are following and trusting the Spirit, there is no reason to feel disappointed by this postponement. If they accept your offer to return, then you have a definite follow-up visit. This too is a matter for prayer. Pray for the family that you will be visiting. Ask the Spirit to prepare you to represent the friendship of Christ when you return.

Likewise, when you meet a family that is immediately open to your visit, stay calm and follow the Spirit. Even though this is the first full visit of the evening, don't get carried away by the appearance of immediate results. This may be a divine appointment, but remember that your purpose in every visit is to build a relationship of genuine care in the name of Christ. The Spirit brought you to this place, so listen to the Spirit's guidance. Focus on loving this family that God has arranged for you to meet. Get to know them as people — their interests and needs — and let yourself be known by them. Remember that your relationship is just beginning. Don't stay too long.

A family like this may tell you that they will definitely be at worship and church school on the following Sunday. Let them know that you would be delighted to see them there, but don't dwell on this alone. Don't focus simply on whether or not they show up at church. Few people will begin to attend the services of a congregation after only one visit in their home. Keep in mind that you have been used by the Spirit in a wonderful way and that through you this family has experienced the love and caring of Jesus Christ. That is your joy and celebration. After a very friendly time with them you will say goodnight and move on.

If you were evaluating this night of visitation according to some standards of immediate results, you might conclude that little of any real importance took place. You were turned away at several houses. No one had a life-changing experience before your very eyes. Even those who welcomed your visit did not make the kind of commitment that you can report as an assured result.

Viewed through the eyes of the Spirit, however, some very important things have been set in motion, not the least of which is your own sensitivity to the importance of prayer in following the Holy Spirit. As you and your team continue to go out and to visit in this way, a change will begin to take place in your ministry area. You will establish a *power of presence*. Even those who reject your visit will know you from now on. They will also recall your friendliness, though they may have treated you in a less than friendly manner. Slowly but surely, the people of your ministry area will spread the word themselves, and you will be surprised at how the Spirit opens the way to relationships that you had not even considered.

Just imagine: Next door to the house where you had your first full visit of the evening, there was a teenage girl swinging on a porch swing. She saw your team walking down the street and thought you were sales people. That night, long after you had already gone home, she picked up the phone and called her girlfriend, the daughter of the family you visited. Her girlfriend told her that you were not sales people; you were from the local United Methodist church. She also said that you were very friendly and not pushy. This impresses the girl who was swinging on the porch and she tells her parents about your visit. Her parents can hardly believe someone from a United Methodist church is out making calls on strangers in the neighborhood. They are delighted because they both grew up as Methodists but have been inactive for years. As this family prepares for bed, those parents say to each other, "I wonder if they'll call here on us? I hope so. I would love to have someone invite me to church."

In this way, visitation teams become part of the landscape, establishing a power of presence in a ministry area. The positive effects of your presence and witness minister in many ways long after you are physically gone from the area. The Holy Spirit multiplies efforts in this way beyond our greatest imaginations. It happens in profound ways.

The very next week your team walks up to the door of the home where the girl lives who was swinging. You ring the doorbell and, as you make introductions, the man of the house waves his hand and smiles. "I know who you are. Our neighbors told us about you. Please come in. We've been hoping you would call here."

Power of presence is a wonderful phenomenon that happens in every ministry area. The only thing we need to concentrate on is being faithful and caring for those we meet under the guidance of the Holy Spirit. Follow the Spirit, pray, and move out beyond the walls.

Part
Two

Introduction to Training Sessions

Welcome to the session-by-session training materials for Lifestyle Relational Evangelism. These training sessions are based on the background and information provided in the first part of this book. There are six training sessions in all. Each session focuses on a specific dimension of LRE as described in Part One. By using these training materials you will be able to build a practical and unified ministry of LRE in your congregation.

LRE is usually started in a congregation by two or three committed laypersons who have become convinced that this model of evangelism is right for their local church (see Part One, Chapter 4). Furthermore, only as these leaders themselves become experienced in the vision and actual practice of LRE are they equipped and qualified to invite others to join them in training for ministry. The training of the initial leaders may take place either as a matter of self-education and experience — using this manual and going out on visits with one or two others — or it may be enhanced by calling on leaders from other congregations who have already begun a ministry of LRE (see below). In either case, as a leader, you should not try to use these training materials in your congregation until you have read this entire book and followed the practical steps outlined in Chapter 4. (Special instructions are included in Appendix A on how local chapters of United Methodist Men can sponsor LRE.)

Once you have an initial group of trained leaders, you are ready to begin recruiting others to join you in ministry (see Chapter 4). At that point, these training modules will assure that you are able to cover all of the basic foundations of the LRE ministry and to effectively communicate these to the members of your congregation who join and support you in ministry. (Note: You will need at least six people — two teams — in order to effectively use some of the team exercises that are described in later sessions.)

Training Schedule Options

Training modules can be scheduled in a variety of ways. The schedule that you decide to use will depend in large measure on the needs and resources of your congregation. For example, if you decide with a few other interested leaders to train yourselves, you may want to use the "Weeknight Study Model," the "Sunday Study and Weeknight Implementation Model," or the "Group Retreat Model." On the other hand, if your initial leadership team decides to seek additional training from outside sources, then you may want to consider the "Basic LRE Training: Mini-Weekend Model." Let's look now at each of these in more detail.

The Weeknight Study Model

This model calls for a six-week course in the principles of LRE. Study sessions are held on the same night each week, each session lasting for approximately one hour. At the end of six weeks, participants continue to meet weekly as visitation teams going out into the homes of their ministry areas.

The Sunday Study and Weeknight Implementation Model

This model calls for a more integrated approach to training and implementation. Trainees meet together for six weeks on Sunday morning or Sunday evening as part of a special study group in order to work through the training modules session by session. At the same time, or perhaps a week or two after training begins, trainees begin going out with experienced visitation teams for "on-the-job" training. One trainee is placed with two trained persons on each team. Trainees might serve, for example, in the role of recorder or supporter. At the end of six weeks, trainees would be organized into their own teams for regular ongoing visitation. This approach offers trainees more experience in the field prior to having a leadership role on a team. This model also requires that organizers plan ahead in order to coordinate schedules with team members who are already trained.

The Congregational Retreat Model

This model calls for opening basic training in LRE to the whole congregation. Therefore, it also requires more advanced planning and preparation. The pioneers of LRE in each congregation should plan to use the "Weeknight Study Model" or the "Sunday Study and Weeknight Implementation Model" with a small group of leaders before offering a congregation-wide training retreat. This will enable local leaders to structure the retreat in a more effective way. Once your core of leaders has experienced training in one of the other models, they will know how to use this book in a retreat setting. Be creative, but be sure to include all the topics in the sessions, even on a retreat weekend.

The Mini-Weekend Model: Basic Training in LRE

This model calls for a concentrated weekend event planned and conducted in coordination with an LRE Instructor and a team of lay trainers from outside the congregation. Instructors and training teams for such events are drawn from congregations that already have LRE in place. As a result, the training process benefits from a wider base of experience. This also gives new meaning to the term *connectionalism* that we in the United Methodist tradition claim as one of our strengths. A weekend event usually includes at least three components:

1. MOTIVATION: Through worship and celebration services, the laity of the local church are moved to become involved in the ministry of LRE.

2. EDUCATION: Through a variety of teaching methods such as lecture, role play, small groups, panel discussion, and video, the laity of the congregation receive extensive training in the vision and methods of LRE.

3. EXPERIENCE: The Instructor and training team also lead the laity of the congregation in making actual visits into the homes of their ministry area, and in setting up an adequate administrative system for purposes of follow-up and regular visitation once the weekend is over.

The Mini-Weekend Model has several advantages. For one thing, it enables the lay members in training to receive immediate "on-the-job" experience with persons (lay and clergy) who have considerable background in LRE. Likewise, since outside trainers are usually housed and fed in the homes of the laypersons receiving the training, the two groups have considerable time for informal conversation. New friendships often form in this context, and seasoned trainers have an opportunity to ease the natural fears of new trainees.

A basic schedule for the Mini-Weekend Model is provided in Appendix B (page 123). This includes a general description of sessions and goals for two days of training — beginning on Friday evening and concluding on Saturday evening. LRE Instructors and trainers are also available for longer training events where this is possible — for example, Friday evening through Sunday morning, or Sunday morning through Tuesday evening. Indeed, training events of longer duration have been conducted effectively in congregations from California to New York, from Wyoming to Georgia. If you would like to receive more information about how to schedule a training event in LRE for your congregation, district, or annual conference, you may call the home office of Proactive Evangelism Ministries, Inc. office and fax at 1-404-949-9674, or contact a leadership team through the following address:

Rev. James W. (Jim) Hollis
Proactive Evangelism Ministries, Inc.
6800 Green Oak Drive
Douglasville, GA 30135-4553

You may also reach Hollis at the following number: CompuServe Mail: 71477, 112.

Each of the models outlined above has certain advantages. Each congregation should choose the model that is best suited to its own needs and resources. What is more, these models are not the only possibilities for implementation of LRE in your local church. This resource can be used in a variety of ways suited to your situation. Therefore, do not feel bound to follow only one of these possible models. Do what you feel will work best in your congregation. The possibilities are virtually endless, yet it is very important to the success and effectiveness of this ministry to receive proper training. The staff at the home office of Proactive Evangelism Ministries, Inc. is available to come to your conference, district, or local church to carry out a custom-designed training event based solely on your group's needs and desires. Jim Hollis and trained laity have led training experiences with pastors' groups also. Models for training at an Annual Conference, District, or Pastors' Retreat are available upon request. Above all, do it more than you talk about it. Move out beyond the walls.

SESSION 1
Biblical Foundations

Lifestyle Relational Evangelism is based on a biblical model of building lasting, caring relationships with others. Biblical evangelism focuses on discipleship as a process, not on "getting decisions" or other kinds of immediate results. This model of evangelism is not, however, widely understood today. Therefore, we need to examine biblical evangelism in some detail even as we overcome certain stereotypes.

Participants should have read Part One, Chapters 1 and 2 in preparation for this session. They should be encouraged in this session to talk openly about some of their own preconceived stereotypes concerning evangelism. This is certainly an appropriate session for humor. All activities can be completed in one hour, unless your group wants to take more time on some of the exercises.

Purposes of Session 1

- To present a clear picture of the biblical basis for the ministry of LRE
- To help participants recognize some false images of evangelism
- To enable participants to begin to get to know each and to work together

Materials Needed

- Bibles for each participant (preferably one's own)
- Notebooks for making notes during the session
- Pencils or pens

❖ Outline for Session 1 ❖

1. Getting Focused *(5 minutes)*

2. Opening Devotion *(5 minutes)*

3. Biblical Evangelism *(30 minutes)*

4. Following Christ *(10 minutes)*

5. Group Reflection *(5 minutes)*

6. Preparing for Next Session *(2 minutes)*

7. Closing Prayer *(3 minutes)*

---

1. Help everyone focus on the topic of evangelism and the ministry of LRE by calling the group to order and reading the following reflection. After the reading, invite participants to discuss their questions or insights about it.

> *Life is very hectic. Hurry itself seems necessary, but hurry is not an answer, for it in itself can be a source of spiritual despair. Focus is important. With proper focus we can grow spiritually. As we take time now to slow down and focus, we hear Jesus calling us to be involved in evangelism ministry, but what motive does <u>he</u> give us for doing evangelism? What is the biblical purpose of doing evangelism today? We know that the Lord wants us to share our faith, yet he never tells us to impose our faith on others. And so we ask him, "Lord, give us discernment to know the difference."*

2. Now lead the class in opening prayer. Emphasize the centrality of prayer in this ministry at every level, and invite the members of the class to share their prayer concerns with one another. Instruct them to record prayer concerns in their notebooks so they can pray for one another during the week. Close this devotional time by inviting the class to read aloud together the following prayer.

> *Lord Jesus, we come asking you to minister to the concerns we have shared today. Precious Lord, we come asking for our hearts to be warmed with the presence of your love. We are a hurried people. We are here to listen to your word and we ask you to help us apply your word to our hearts. Help us see ourselves in the scriptures that we study today, rather than just seeing them as a part of history. Send the power of your Holy Spirit upon us, gathered here out of love for you. Help us focus clearly on what you would have us hear during this time together; for we pray in your name, dear Jesus. Amen.*

3. Evangelism is central in the Bible, but how does the biblical understanding of evangelism relate to our lives and ministries? Help participants explore this question by reading the following biblical passages together. Divide the class into small groups (three persons in each group), and instruct the groups to examine each of the following passages, answering the questions that appear with each passage. One person in each group should serve as a recorder, keeping notes of the group's responses. When the groups have had an opportunity to examine all of the passages, bring the class back together as a whole and invite the recorder from each group to share the responses.

Matthew 28:16-20
- What does Jesus' statement about having "all authority" mean for us today? What difference does this statement make in the way we understand his call to go and make disciples?
- What is the relationship between "making a decision for Christ" and "making a disciple for Christ"? Why does this matter in visitation ministry?
- When people resist the call to evangelism today, what negative stereotypes might they have in mind? How does Jesus' "Great Commission" change the negative stereotype of evangelism?

Luke 10:1-3, 16-23

- What kind of people were the seventy that Jesus appointed to go? How do you think you would have felt to be chosen as one of the seventy?
- What are some specific signs in your community that the harvest is plentiful today?
- What implications does this have for visitation ministry?
- Why did Jesus refocus the joy of the seventy as they returned from their mission? What does this tell you about the source of lasting motivation for laborers going into the harvest?

Revelation 12:7-12

- What are some specific ways in which Satan deceives and accuses people today? Why are Christians sometimes skeptical about discussing this topic?
- How would you respond if a visitor came to you after the morning worship service and said, "Please explain to me what the pastor meant when she talked about "power in the blood."
- The pastor calls you tonight and says, "I have been praying about having more personal testimonies in our worship service. Would you please share this Sunday at 11:00 worship on the topic, *Living the Abundant Life in Christ?*" Honestly, how would this make you feel? What would you talk about if you shared?

4. Now move to another level of interaction with the scripture by inviting participants to put the meaning of Philippians 2:5-11 into their own words. Continue to work in small groups of three. Instruct each group to read the passage from Philippians, to briefly discuss its meaning, and then to paraphrase it in terms and images that are familiar today. In order to enrich their paraphrases, invite groups to consider what it would mean in their own congregation and in their own neighborhoods to follow this exhortation completely. What will it mean, for example, to "empty" ourselves or to take "the form of a slave" in these settings? When the small groups have completed their work, invite them to come back together with the whole class and to share their paraphrases with one another.

5. Invite participants to evaluate the session they have just completed by discussing the following questions. You might keep track of brief responses by recording them on a sheet of newsprint where everyone can see.
   - What is the most helpful thing I have learned during this session? What has been the most interesting topic or scripture passage?
   - How will what I have learned help me grow spiritually closer to Jesus Christ?
   - What would I like for the class to study more closely?

6. Preparing for Next Session:
   - Read Part One, Chapter 3 before coming to class for the next session.
   - Make a personal list of people you know in each of the six categories described in Chapter 3, and begin praying for these people by name.
   - Pray during the coming week for the members of your LRE ministry group, believing that the Lord will multiply your prayers and efforts in this undertaking.

7. Close this session by inviting all participants to read together the following psalm.

> *May God be gracious to us and bless us and make his face to shine upon us, that your way may be known upon earth, your saving power among all nations. Let the peoples praise you, O God; let all the peoples praise you. Let the nations be glad and sing for joy, for you judge the peoples with equity and guide the nations upon earth. Let the peoples praise you, O God; let all the peoples praise you. The earth has yielded its increase; God, our God, has blessed us. May God continue to bless us; let all the ends of the earth revere him.*

SESSION 2
Meeting Needs

Every congregation is surrounded by people with many different kinds of needs. Some people are totally unconnected with the church. Others have become inactive, often due to some conflict in the past. Still others have felt that they were unable to be involved either because of illness, or age, or simply because they were new in the community. Christ calls us as the church to reach out to all of these needs. In order to reach out in ways that are truly helpful, however, we must understand more about the needs of each of those we seek to serve.

In preparation for this session, participants should read Part One, Chapter 3. In this session we shall examine the distinct needs of six groups of people as described in Chapter 3, and we shall work together to compile a master list of people in and around our own congregation who have needs such as these. This list will become, in turn, an outline of ministry possibilities for the congregation's LRE ministry. All activities can be completed in one hour unless your group wants to take more time on some exercises.

Purposes of Session 2

- To give participants a clear understanding of six groups of people who can become the focus of ministry in their local church
- To begin to prioritize needs for ministry action

Materials Needed

- Six sheets of newsprint for the leader to use in Exercise 4
- A current copy of the church directory for each participant
- Notebooks for all participants

❖ Outline for Session 2 ❖

1. Getting Focused *(5 minutes)*

2. Opening Prayer *(5 minutes)*

3. Six Ministry Groups *(30 minutes)*

4. Making a Master List *(10 minutes)*

5. Group Reflection *(5 minutes)*

6. Preparing for Next Session *(2 minutes)*

7. Closing Prayer *(3 minutes)*

1. Help class members begin focusing their thoughts by calling the class to order and reading the following reflection. After the reading, invite the participants to share their thoughts and questions in response to the reflection.

> *As we gather for this session, we are surrounded by persons who live in our community — all of whom have needs, many of whom are in great pain. They are often lonely, hurting, empty, hopeless, and unloved — even by members of their own families. We are called to <u>be</u> the church of Jesus Christ in the world. Jesus wants us to reach out to this world of needs, to touch persons where they live, even in the midst of their pain. It is not enough to have nice signs pointing to the church, or great programs for those who attend, or wonderful services for active members. We are sent. Why are we reluctant to go? Is there any greater ministry for us?*

2. Now lead the class in a time of opening prayer. Re-emphasize the centrality of prayer in this ministry at every level, and invite participants to share their prayer concerns with one another. Instruct participants to continue to record prayer concerns in their notebooks so they can pray for one another during the week. When all have shared their concerns, invite the class to read aloud together the following prayer.

> *Lord Jesus, we praise you that we have come to know you as our personal Lord and Savior. We are in awe that you call us to be the church. We are not comfortable with stepping out into the unknown. We feel the risk. We sense the uncertainty. We are afraid. Calm our fears and cast away our anxiety. Convince our hearts that some of our best friends are yet to be made — people who live "out there," beyond the walls of our church building. Send us to them with your love, in your power, and filled with your grace. Make us sensitive to the needs of those around us and around our church, for we pray in your name, dear Jesus. Amen.*

3. Help the members of the class begin to get inside the needs of the six ministry groups described in Chapter 3. Divide the class into small groups of three. Instruct each group to read the following first person descriptions and to spend about five minutes with each description discussing the questions that follow. The task of reader can circulate among the members of the group, but each reader should read as though he or she is the person being described. (Check with the groups at five-minute intervals to be sure they are moving along to the next description.)

The Unchurched
> *"My family and I are nice people. I own a small manufacturing company that employs about fifty people. My wife is a science teacher at the local college. Our two small children, ages seven and four, are very happy. We have a beautiful home, three nice cars, and a cabin in the mountains where we love to spend the weekends relaxing. We don't go to church. We believe in God, but we have never been into institutionalized religion."*

- What needs might this family have that do not show up in the description?
- You are on a ministry team assigned to their area. You have met this family and they were polite to your team. What does the Christian faith have to offer this family?

- What are some important things we can do to build a meaningful relationship with this family?

Inactive Members

"Our family used to go to your church. When our children were still in school, we were involved in almost everything. My husband and I were on committees and spent at least two nights a week at the church building, in addition to worship and Sunday school. My mother, who lives in a neighboring state, became very ill with a serious heart condition. The kids graduated and left. We lost touch with the church after a time, spending most weekends with my mother. When that started, our friends just quit calling us as much. The only time we've seen anyone from the church in the last ten months was when a team came to our door making their annual pitch for money. We feel hurt and forgotten."

- This couple was mentioned in your Sunday school class this past Sunday. The comment was made, "I doubt if they will be back." What is your response to this?
- What is really going on with this family? What are their needs? Why are they hurting and feeling forgotten?
- How will we win this family back to our church? What, from their perspective, is the most important thing that we can do?

Moving Members

"My family and I have been a vital part of our church for the last three years. I have worked as children's coordinator and helped organize a new preschool ministry. My husband has served on the trustees and helped to landscape the church grounds. He works for a national company and has been transferred to another state. Our house has not sold. He had to report to the new job in six weeks. That was three months ago. The kids and I have been here all that time trying to sell the house so we can be together. We see each other some on weekends. At first, our fellow church members were emotional about our leaving. Then, as time passed, we seemed to just be 'out of sight and out of mind.' I hope we will never have to go through this pain again."

- This family was not intentionally forgotten, but they may be in danger of becoming inactive. How would you describe the pattern of events that led to their situation?
- How could the local church have ministered to their needs more effectively?

Ministry Referrals

"Do we know where First United Methodist is? Of course, we do. Our son Paul is in the Scout troop there. We take him there every Tuesday night. We don't go to worship or Sunday school because Sundays are a catch-up day for our family. Some Sundays we even take in a ballgame or other special event. Paul has asked about going to church, but we haven't gone yet."

- What kind of witness has First United Methodist made to this family? How does the family feel about the church as a result of this witness?
- How can we reach out to this family? What are some specific things we might do to extend the fellowship of the church to them?

- If we do not take the initiative in reaching out to this family, is it likely that they will ever walk into worship as visitors?

Worship Visitors

"This seems like a nice church. People are fairly friendly. Someone even spoke to us and gave us a worship bulletin as we entered. We're just visiting congregations in the area. We're in our thirties with two small children. We're not sure where we'll end up, but it will probably be somewhere that we feel comfortable and where it will be a good environment for our family."

- What is this family searching for in their sampling of congregations?
- What do they mean by the word *comfortable*? How important is this to visitors and how do we make this happen?
- What are some of the needs of this family?

The Elderly and Homebound

"I am a widow. My husband outran me to glory about twelve years ago. I live here in this little house we built in 1935. I can see the steeple of our church from my breakfast room window. We had so many bright years there. I guess I've served in about all of the offices in the church in my day. For the last few years I haven't been able to get out except to go to the doctor. The pastor comes by about every other month to see me. He's very friendly but I know he's busy. I read the newsletter at least three times each week to try to stay in touch. I wish I could go to church."

- If this woman is not able to go to church, what are some ways the church could come to her?
- What would it take for our church to be consistently involved in ministry with the sick and homebound?
- What role do laity have in this tremendous need?

4. Now invite the members of the class to work together in composing a master list of people they know in or around the ministry area of your congregation who have needs like those described. Post the sheets of newsprint (prepared in advance) around the room, and invite everyone to move about among these lists, adding names to the appropriate lists and checking to see what names others have put on the lists. This is an opportunity to put real names with the real needs already described. After all the names are listed, invite the class to look at all the lists together. Remember, these lists can now serve as the foundation of your new ministry of LRE.

- Which lists are the longest? Which are the shortest? Why?
- On the basis of these lists, what does the class feel might be a good place to focus your first efforts in visitation?
- Do any of the lists suggest that a special LRE group should be started that meets on a day or at a time different from the regular visitation schedule (e.g., a ministry to the homebound that meets on a weekday morning)?

5. Invite the members of the class to reflect on their learnings in this session by answering the following questions.

- What is the most helpful thing I have learned during this session? What has been the most interesting topic or question?
- How will what I have learned help me grow spiritually closer to Jesus Christ?
- What would I like the group to study more closely?

6. Preparing for Next Session:

- **Participants:** Read Part One, Chapter 5. Pay special attention to what it means to be part of an LRE team. Ponder the following questions:

  — Of the three roles (leader, supporter, recorder), which would I best fulfill and why?
  — Which would be the most challenging for me?

- Go to the city or county courthouse and obtain the most detailed map possible of your own street and residential area. Begin to think about how a team might use this map to keep track of visits in its ministry area. Bring the map and your ideas to the next session.

- **Trainers:** Based on your thoughts at the time of recruiting, and on subsequent experiences thus far in the training, begin to refine your thoughts about the composition of teams. Which trainees might work together most effectively as teams? Which team members may be able to visit in the area of their own residences? Which may need to visit in other areas? You will gather more information on some of these questions at the next session with a view to coordinating final team assignments by Session 6.

- If you do not already have one, you will also need to create a map of the total ministry area of your congregation, including the natural dividing lines for team ministry areas as described in Chapter 5.

7. Close the session by inviting the members of the class to read aloud together the following prayer:

   Lord Jesus, minister through us to those whose names we have written and remembered today. May they not be forgotten, even as you have never forgotten us. Send the power of your Holy Spirit upon us that we may become strong in ministry for you. In your name we ask this prayer. Amen.

SESSION 3
Organizing Teams

Team ministry is the best way for a congregation to fulfill the spiritual vision of LRE in its total ministry area. Teams allow the congregation to be systematic in going out to visit and in keeping track of responses for follow-up calls. Teams also provide enormous support and spiritual growth for their members. Organizing teams, however, takes a good deal of time, forethought, and planning. A number of issues must be raised and solved: Who will be on a team? Where will they visit? What is the schedule for visitation? The solution to these issues, furthermore, requires the coordinated efforts of all concerned — trainers, administrators, and team members.

In preparation for this session, participants should have read Part One, Chapter 5 on the organization of ministry teams. During this session, trainers will lead participants in organizing ministry teams. The composition of these teams may change in some details as trainers make adjustments for individual needs in the weeks ahead, yet team identity and cohesion are goals that need to be reached as soon as possible. In this session, team members will also begin to imagine the conduct and manner of an actual visit and to discuss their potential team ministry areas. All activities can be completed in an hour and a half unless the teams want to take more time on certain exercises.

Purposes of Session 3

- To help participants discover the importance of being part of a ministry team in LRE
- To give participants a clear understanding of what takes place on a typical evening of visitation
- To discuss potential team ministry areas

❖ Outline for Session 3 ❖

1. Getting Focused *(5 minutes)*

2. Opening Prayer *(5 minutes)*

3. Organizing Teams *(15 minutes)*

4. Maps and Ministry Areas *(20 minutes)*

5. Role Play of an Actual Visit *(30 minutes)*

6. Group Reflection *(7 minutes)*

7. Preparing for Next Session *(5 minutes)*

8. Closing Prayer *(3 minutes)*

Materials and Preparation Needed

- A *roster* of ministry teams for Exercise 3 prepared in advance
- Invite the members of one of these teams (three persons) to come to the session dressed in three different ways: 1) extremely casual (almost sloppy), 2) casual (slacks and shirt, or a casual dress or pantsuit), and 3) formal (suit and tie or formal dress). These three will represent the visitation team for the role play in Exercise 4.
- A detailed map of the *total* ministry area of your congregation for Exercise 5
- Notebooks and pencils/pens for all participants

1. Help everyone focus on the theme for this session by calling the class to order and reading aloud the following reflection. After the reading, invite participants to discuss their thoughts and questions about the reflection.

   > *Jesus called twelve disciples. These twelve worked together with Jesus as a team. At first, there was much awkwardness. It took time for them to get to know each other. Each had personal strengths and weaknesses. Jesus built on their strengths and looked beyond their weaknesses. As we seek to join in ministry teams together, we must do no less. The Holy Spirit can build two or three people into an effective ministry team. Without the Spirit, we can only fake it for a time.*

2. Lead the class in opening prayer. Continue to emphasize the centrality of prayer and to invite participants to share their prayer concerns with one another — keeping track of concerns in their notebooks. Close the prayer time by inviting the class to read aloud together the following prayer.

   > *Lord Jesus, make us instruments of your peace, love, and grace. We pray as we become ministry teams that you would bond us together in the power of your Holy Spirit. May we be sent forth in your name and love. In your name we ask these blessings. Amen.*

3. Now lead the class in forming ministry teams. The roster you prepared in advance is very important at this point. Your roster should reflect your own best thoughts about the personalities and styles of the members of the class. Try to place team members according to the following characteristics:

   - One person for each team who is outspoken and outgoing (team leader)
   - One person who is helpful and encouraging (support person)
   - One person who is more reserved but a good listener (recorder)

   You may either post a copy of the roster at the front of the room or hand out copies to all participants. In any event, ask participants to find the members of their team and to sit together. You may need to assure some members at this point that team assignments are provisional. It will be possible *following the session* to make adjustments in team composition based on individual needs. Most participants, however, will see the wisdom of their assignments and will be happy to begin working as teams. It may also be helpful to remind everyone that part of the excitement of LRE is the opportunity to know and work with a wide range of people in your own congregation. Invite the newly formed teams to discuss the following questions:

- What are the obvious strengths of this team?
- What things do we have in common as team members?
- What aspects or features of church life would each of us be most comfortable discussing on an actual visit?
- What roles would each of us like to have on the team? How do we feel about everyone eventually serving as leader, support person, and recorder?

4. Now invite the newly formed teams to begin thinking with each other about how to effectively *use* maps for the conduct of ministry in specific geographic regions. Ask for volunteers to hold up the maps they brought with them to the session, to explain how and where they got them, and to note any special features of the maps procured. Next, lead the class in an open discussion of the skills required to effectively use a map in ministry:

- What do lines, squares, and numbers on the map represent?
- How will teams mark their maps in order to keep track of visits?
- What supplies are most useful in marking maps for long-term ministry?

To close this exercise, turn the attention of the class to the map of the congregation's *total* ministry area that you acquired in advance. If your LRE ministry has been organized for some time, this map may already include a number of well-defined team ministry areas. If you are just starting out, some of the team ministry areas may still seem provisional. In either case, help the newly formed teams recognize how individual team ministry areas relate to the congregation's total ministry area, and let them know that ministry area assignments will be made in Session 6. (Note: The focus of this exercise is on *how* to use maps, not on *where* to assign specific teams. The latter is an administrative function that will usually require more time and reflection than is available in this exercise.)

5. Now invite the class to relax as you enter into another phase of training by means of dramatic role play. The cast for the role play will involve two of your newly formed teams: one to represent the visiting team (dressed in different attires), the other to represent the family or household being visited. Your cast will need some background, but be sure to give each team only those details that pertain to its part. (Cast members can also use the materials on role playing in Appendix D for additional ideas.)

DETAILS FOR THE TEAM MAKING THE CALL

You are a visitation team from First United Methodist Church. You are out to love and care for persons who are unchurched in your ministry area. You have not yet met the family you are visiting this evening. (*You have no lines or script other than to be yourselves. Act just as you think you would if you were actually making this visit. Choose a team leader, a support person, and a recorder before you start your visit.*)

The background information for the family being visited requires a bit more detail. Instead of scripting all of this, however, allow the team playing this part to fill in the following outline. In this way, the visiting team will truly be in the position of trying to get to know a family whose background is as yet unknown.

DETAILS FOR THE FAMILY BEING VISITED

You are a family. You moved to this area _____ months ago. You are (*married, divorced, widowed, roommates*). The head of the household works for _____.
The spouse or roommate (*if there is one*) is looking for a job and works with (*computers, law enforcement, white collar, teaching, other*). You have _____ children in the home, and they are _____ old. Your (*mother, father, sister, brother*) has just discovered some very bad news medically. It is that your _____ has _____. Your attitude about this is _____

_____

(*With this script in hand, your task is to act as if you are the members of this family. These are the needs the visiting team will be trying to discover as they make their call.*)

Before starting the role play, encourage all participants to be creative, yet to act naturally in their roles. Try to keep things as realistic as possible. Avoid obvious slapstick humor to impress the audience, as this would *not* happen on a good visit. Plan for the role play to last about ten to fifteen minutes. While cast members are preparing their parts (allow about three minutes for this), instruct the rest of the class to please remain quiet and to take notes about the visit as the role play is in progress. At the close of the role play, be sure to affirm the cast members for taking part, and invite the class as a whole to discuss the questions given below. The role play can start when the visiting team knocks on the door and enters the home of the family being visited.

Role Play Discussion Questions
- What needs were discovered during the visit? List these on a sheet of newsprint or a chalkboard.
- Were any needs of the family being visited *not* discovered?
- Was the call friendly and positive, or was it stressful? Why?
- How did the different dress styles make you feel as you watched the visit taking place?
- If you were part of the visiting team, what would you want to do differently next time?
- If you were part of the family being visited, what would you like the visitors to do differently next time?

6. Ask the members of the class to reflect on their learnings during this session by answering the following questions.

   • What is the most helpful thing I learned during this session? What was the most interesting topic or exercise?
   • How will what I have learned help me grow spiritually closer to Christ?
   • What would I like the class to study more closely?

7. Preparing for Next Session:

   • **Participants:** Read Part One, Chapter 6. In particular, pay close attention to the details of the three different kinds of visits: first-time visit, follow-up visit, and casual acquaintance visit. Reflect on being part of these visits. What is the most important thing to remember about each kind of visit? Why?

   • **Team leaders of newly formed teams:** During the week, discuss with the members of your team the following questions related to a visitation schedule. Write your names and responses to the questions on a sheet of notebook paper, and turn this in at the next session. (Note: Some of these matters may already have been discussed when participants were recruited for training. If so, simply indicate your understanding of the schedule that has been agreed, and note any new or special concerns that may need consideration. Reading material related to a schedule is in Chapter 5, pages 43-44.)

     — What day(s) of the week would be best for our team to visit?
     — What time(s) of day or evening would be best for us to visit?
     — Does our team have any special requests to make with regard to the order or length of a typical visitation schedule?
     — Would our team like to be considered for a special assignment related to a particular ministry need — for example, the need to call on worship visitors within forty-eight hours after their attendance?

   • **Trainers:** Begin working in earnest to identify persons with administrative gifts (if you do not already have administrators in place). Trainers will need to work with administrators in the next two weeks to finalize team assignments, ministry areas, and the regular schedule for weekly visitation. These plans should be coordinated with special needs as noted by participants so that a working plan can be announced in Session 6.

8. Lead the class in a time of closing prayer. Invite leaders and members of your new LRE teams to pray for one another and for the future of your ministry together.

SESSION 4
The Great Adventure of Visitation

In order to prepare for the adventure of visitation, teams need to get inside the anatomy of a typical visit. What, however, is a "typical" visit? How might the conversation of a first-time visit compare with that of a follow-up visit, or a casual acquaintance visit? As teams build their skills in response to these questions, they will also come to realize that no two visits are ever exactly alike. The people we visit are individuals with a great variety of needs, interests, and backgrounds. As a consequence, the most important thing of all for LRE teams to know and understand is their central purpose: to build relationships, to meet needs, and to represent the love of Christ.

In preparation for this session, participants should have read Part One, Chapter 6 on the nature of different kinds of visits. During this session, teams will be invited to take part in (or to observe) role plays of a first-time visit and a follow-up visit. Teams will also practice writing thank you notes. In addition, for those teams who want to extend their time by about twenty minutes, a role play for a casual acquaintance visit is included. All activities can be completed in one hour unless teams want to spend extra time on one or more of the role plays.

Purposes of Session 4

- To give teams an opportunity to experience in role play the adventure of making various kinds of visits
- To help team members get in touch with and overcome some of the fears or unrealistic expectations that they may have about visiting
- To help teams focus again on the paramount importance of building relationships and meeting needs
- To help teams anticipate the joy of calling on others through visitation

❖ **Outline for Session 4** ❖

1. Getting Focused *(5 minutes)*
2. Opening Prayer *(5 minutes)*
3. First-Time Visit Role Play *(20 minutes)*
4. Follow-Up Visit Role Play *(15 minutes)*
   (Optional: Casual Acquaintance Role Play, *15 minutes)*
5. Thank You Notes *(5 minutes)*
6. Group Reflection *(5 minutes)*
7. Preparing for Next Session *(3 minutes)*
8. Closing Prayer *(2 minutes)*

Materials Needed

- A few comfortable chairs to use in role playing
- Newsprint or chalkboard for registering responses in group discussion
- Blank sheets of paper for writing thank you notes
- Notebooks for each participant
- Pencils and pens

1. Help teams focus on the theme for this session by calling the class to order and reading the following reflection. After the reading, invite the members of the class to share their responses and questions.

   No one can predict how another person will respond to a ministry team that comes to visit. Some people have a background full of pain in relation to the church. Others are indifferent. Some already belong to another congregation. Still others do not belong anywhere, but they have been thinking about the need to grow spiritually. Foreknowledge of another person's background is not necessary for LRE teams, however, for they go out with one purpose in mind: to build caring relationships in the name of Christ regardless of the responses or reactions they may encounter.

2. Lead the class (or ask one of the team leaders to lead) in a time of opening prayer. Share prayer concerns, keep notes in your notebooks, and read aloud together 1 Corinthians 13. Close your prayer time by reading aloud together the following prayer.

   Lord Jesus, on our own we cannot really love you in the way that you intended. Give us the fullness of your Holy Spirit that your love may fill us and spill over to those around us. May your passion for reaching out to the lost and needy become for us a fire in our bones. Send us forth in the power and authority that are yours alone as King of Kings and Lord of Lords. In your name. Amen.

3. Now invite the class to engage in a role play of a first-time visit. Make this an enjoyable learning experience. Choose two teams: one to play the household being visited, the other for the visiting LRE team. Choose people to participate who will be enthusiastic about their involvement, but not too humorous in acting. Give the teams about three minutes to review the background for their parts. The background for the visiting team is given below. Instruct the team to be visited to use the framed outline on page 98 and the materials in Appendix D to develop identities for their roles.

   While the teams are preparing, ask for volunteers to arrange the front of the room with chairs to represent a typical living room situation. The role play itself should last about ten minutes. This will leave about seven minutes for discussion. Remind everyone that you will be timing the role play. Start the discussion after the role play by affirming all who took part. (Role playing is more difficult in some ways than making an actual call where one does not have an audience.) The questions at the end of the role play are intended to sharpen the discussion, but be sure to share critiques as "additional ministry techniques or strategies" rather than "what they did wrong." The role play can begin as soon as the visiting team knocks on the door.

DETAILS FOR THE CALLING TEAM

You are a visitation team from your home church, making a first-time visit in your ministry area. You will use your own names and your real identities as you meet this new family. Practice using first names only in introductions at the door. Be natural and attentive to the family you are visiting. Enjoy meeting them and getting to know them. Discover as many needs as possible on this first call. Be certain to get their names and correct mailing address for the newsletter to be mailed to them. *(The recorder can use an Initial Visit Form to record this information even though these forms will not be formally introduced until the next session.)* Begin the role play by knocking on the door. Keep time to ten minutes.

Role Play Discussion Questions
- How would you evaluate the receptivity level of the family being visited on this call? How soon should the team return for a follow-up visit?
- What were the key needs that came out during the visit? (List on newsprint or chalkboard.)
- Did the family have needs that were not discovered?
- What things were said or done by the calling team to contribute to the building of relationships?

4. Instructions for the follow-up role play are similar to those for the first-time visit, only now the visiting team is called to build on the relationship that has already begun. Use the same teams for this role play. Once again, after the role play, discuss the follow-up questions in a way that is mutually constructive.

INSTRUCTIONS FOR FOLLOW-UP TEAM

After your first visit, you evaluated the receptivity level of this family and set a date for a follow-up visit. Now you are returning to make that visit. Everything that you discovered on the first visit needs to be recalled at this time — names, needs, interests, etc. Begin the role play by having a pre-visit briefing about this information in front of the whole class, using the notes your recorder made on the Initial Visit Form. Your purpose on this visit is to deepen your relationship with the members of this family — by responding to a specific need, by pursuing a social relationship (a tennis game, lunch out, going to the mall, etc.), or by some other means. The focus of the visit is *not* on getting this family to the church building. You are there to be the church. If family members say they really meant to come to church, just acknowledge this and immediately move on to deepening your relationship with them. Your recorder can keep notes on this call on a Follow-Up Visit Form. Keep the role play to ten minutes.

INSTRUCTIONS FOR FAMILY RECEIVING THE FOLLOW-UP VISIT

Your situation may not have changed much since your first visit with the ministry team from the church. You may, however, change some details if you wish. Have any of the needs that were mentioned during the first visit changed in any way — for better or for worse? Have any new needs developed that you may feel comfortable mentioning if the visiting team continues to show sensitivity? You may also thank the visiting team for things that have been done since the first visit. Did anyone come to visit a relative in the hospital? Did you receive a note of appreciation after the first visit? Have any of the things that were done or said on the first visit continued to have special meaning for you? If you identify any of these things, express your thanks as you believe an actual family would. (Also, since *you* are creating the memory of these kindnesses *in the role play*, you will need to give the visiting team a moment to recall what they have done.)

Role Play Discussion Questions

- Was making a follow-up visit easier than making the first-time visit? Why or why not?
- What things were done during this visit to enhance and deepen the friendship with the family being visited?
- What other things could have been done on this call?

Optional Casual Acquaintance Call

Instructions for the optional casual acquaintance visit are similar. Since this is not a follow-up call, however, you can choose two new teams to play the roles. Invite the cast members to take a few minutes to consider their parts. They can also use the materials in Appendix D to enhance their roles. Rearrange chairs and other props to suggest a doctor's waiting room. Above all, this role play illustrates that opportunities to reach out with the love of Christ occur every single day in ways that many church members may not have considered. Help the class see how natural and easy it can be to build new friendships — friendships that may last a lifetime and become the foundation for another person to experience the love of Christ. (If you do not use this role play in class, encourage the members of the class to study it on their own.)

DETAILS FOR THE VISITOR

You have come to your doctor's office for a check-up and you are sitting in the waiting room. Others are waiting in the room with you. In general, people are bored; they have nowhere to go. Some may be anxious about what the doctor will tell them. Be natural as you begin a conversation with one of these strangers. Focus the conversation on *his or her* situation, his or her need. Relate to this person. As the conversation develops, share something of your own story — in particular, something that *alludes* to the importance of Christ, the church, or faith in your life. Be careful, however, *not* to use church terms. Pay attention to the stranger's response. Is he or she interested in knowing more about what you mean? (This is often the case.) In any event, continue to be natural, never pushy. Concentrate on his or her needs. Care for this other person as though you were a best friend in this situation.

DETAILS FOR THE PERSON BEING VISITED

You are in a physician's waiting room. You are here to take some tests the doctor has requested because a recent routine physical raised some questions about your health. Use the materials in Appendix D or your own imagination to determine the specific focus of your medical concern. As a result of this concern, you are naturally tense and somewhat worried. At the same time, however, you are more receptive than you have been in a long time to the care and genuine support of others. You have ten minutes before you have to go in to see the doctor.

Role Play Discussion Questions
- How did the person initiating this visit pick up on the needs of this other person? Was this done in a natural way?
- How did the conversation develop to include personal sharing about Christ, the church, or faith? Did this feel natural or pushy?
- What could have been done to make this a more effective visit with this stranger?

5. Now hand out blank sheets of paper and invite everyone in the class to prepare a thank you note to those who were visited in one of the role plays. Let each person choose which role play he or she wants to respond to. Encourage participants to remember the details of the visit, including any interests or needs that might be important to mention in the note. As people finish their notes, ask them to pass them to the front. Share some of these with the class as a whole, and invite the members of the class to comment on the strengths they see in each one. (Participants may sign their notes if they wish.)

6. Ask the members of the class to reflect on their learnings during this session by answering the following questions.

   - What is the most helpful thing I learned during this session? What was the most interesting topic or exercise?
   - How will what I have learned help me grow spiritually closer to Christ?
   - What would I like the class to study more closely?

7. Preparing for Next Session:

   - **Participants:** Read Part One, Chapter 7 on the topic of administration. Pay particular attention to the various forms that are introduced in this chapter.

   - Remember the prayer concerns listed in your notebook

   - **Trainers:** Take up the notes that team leaders collected during the past week related to ideas for the visitation schedule, and continue to work toward finalizing specific team assignments, ministry areas, and the schedule for visitation that you will use for regular visitation.

- Begin to think in earnest about *who* will serve as *administrators*. Keep in mind the special gifts that are required for administration. People with gifts for administration will sometimes not feel called to participate in active visitation. In any event, administration is a full-time job. Therefore, a person should not try to serve as a visitation team member and an administrator at the same time. (If you have persons whose situation has changed in some way since they began this training — so that it may be difficult for them to continue as a team member, consider inviting them to serve in an administrative role.)

- This is also an important time during the training to do some additional group building.* Consider planning a midweek potluck meal before the next session with members of the class, or invite everyone to go out for dessert or coffee after the next session in order to have some more time for informal sharing.

8. Close this session by inviting teams to read aloud together the following prayer.

    God, we know that you give us hundreds of opportunities every day to share your love with those whose paths we encounter. We also know that sharing in this way with them can only happen as all of our actions, attitudes, and words point directly to you. Give us the fullness of your joy as we reach out in your name, in your Spirit, and at your command. In Jesus' name, Amen.

---

*At this point in your ministry development, you may have specific questions or even a few frustrations. If so, feel free to Fax your thoughts to the Office of Proactive Evangelism Ministries, Inc., or send Jim Hollis electronic mail via *CompuServe*. (Fax # 404-949-9674 or CompuServe address for Hollis and staff: 71477, 112.) They will try to respond within 48 hours. Be sure to include either a Fax number or CompuServe address I.D.

SESSION 5
Administering the Movement

Genuine long-term ministry requires effective administration. Ministry teams must be able to keep track of the results and responses of numerous visits with dozens and even hundreds of people over long periods of time. For this purpose LRE congregations have developed a set of basic forms on which to record essential information about each visit. As teams learn to use these forms in coordination with their administrators, the ministry of LRE will grow and flourish in ever deeper ways.

In preparation for this session, participants should have read Part One, Chapter 5 on the ministry of administration. If you already have individuals who have agreed to serve as administrators, introduce them in this session and invite them to help you present the various materials that will be used in the exercises — forms, filing system, etc. This session depends largely on your enthusiasm in presenting the materials outlined. Be sure that you and all others who lead in this session are completely familiar with the materials prior to the session. All activities can be completed in one hour unless teams wish to take more time on a particular exercise.

Purposes of Session 5

- To help all participants understand the primary importance of the ministry of administration in visitation
- To show participants how to keep accurate records in the establishment of relationships
- If possible, to introduce administrators

❖ Outline for Session 5 ❖

1. Getting Focused *(5 minutes)*

2. Opening Prayer *(5 minutes)*

3. Visitation Forms *(15 minutes)*

4. Team Leader's Resource Kit *(10 minutes)*

5. Filing Systems *(15 minutes)*

6. Group Reflection *(5 minutes)*

7. Preparing for Next Session *(2 minutes)*

8. Closing Prayer *(3 minutes)*

Materials Needed

- Copies of all forms (Initial Visit, Follow-Up Visit, and Report) for all participants
- A complete team leader's resource kit as described in Chapter 7 (page 67)
- A few surprise items of a humorous nature (canteen, bandaid, snake-bite kit, etc.) to go into the kit to add some levity to the presentation
- Examples of filing system materials or equipment that you already have available
- Notebooks and pens or pencils

1. Help teams focus on the theme of administration for this session by calling the class to order and reading aloud Acts 6:1-3. Then invite the class to continue listening as you read the following reflection. After the reading, invite participants to share their thoughts in response.

> *Ministry is a level ground. Jesus may send you to preach to a crowd of 5,000 or to spend some time with a lonely widow. Both are equal in the eyes of the One who chose to go to Jerusalem knowing that a cross awaited. As we stand in faith around that cross, we realize that we are all the same height. None is more important. None is less. We are all sinners, depending only on the One who died on the cross and now lives in us. In this light, those who keep records faithfully are just as beautiful as those whose hands knock on doors. We are all individual parts of the Body of Christ. We are all called to ministry. That, my brothers and sisters, is simple servanthood; and it is a key to the joy of the abundant life.*

2. Lead the class in a time of opening prayer. Continue to encourage the members of the class to share prayer concerns with one another and to keep track of special concerns in their notebooks, in order to remember one another in prayer during the week. In addition, for this session, invite everyone to share in a time of directed praise and prayer. Use the following prayer form, and invite all who want to, to share their prayers aloud. Close this time of prayer by reading aloud together the final words of praise and petition.

> *Lord, I thank you for* _____
> *I ask you to help me with* _____
> *Please be close to* _____

> **All:** *We are honored to be called to serve you in all of these ways. Help us, Lord, as we reach out in your name to a hurting world. Amen.*

3. Now introduce the three primary forms that will be used to effectively administer the work of your LRE teams. (If an administrator is available, you might ask him or her to help in presenting these materials.) Begin by handing out copies of the Initial Visit Form to all participants and inviting them to discuss the following questions:

- Why is the question "Are you presently active in a local church?" one of the most important questions on this form?
- What criteria would you use in deciding whether to schedule a follow-up visit, and how soon to schedule it?

Next hand out the Follow-Up Visit Form to all participants and discuss three more questions.

- In comparison to the Initial Visit Form, the Follow-Up Visit Form contains very little information. Why is so little information necessary this time around?
- What are some needs that might be recorded on this form?
- Can you think of examples of personal or confidential information that would not be recorded on the form?

Finally, hand out copies of the Report Session Form to all participants and discuss the following questions:

- Why is accountability important for this ministry? How does this form give us accountability?
- What would be some very positive ways to share the information from the Report Session Forms in the local church?

4. Introduce a working model of the Team Leader's Resource Kit. Remember, this is a special tool kit for this ministry, so be like a little child with a new toy. Make the presentation exciting and fun. Stand in front of the class with the kit on a table where all can see. Talk about the importance of a good quality bag or container. Then go through the items one at a time until you have emptied the bag. Intersperse some humorous items in your presentation. In everything you do, emphasize the following:

- Each team leader should purchase the materials for a kit and keep it stocked at all times.
- Team leaders should carry their kits in their cars at all times in order to be ready to share materials whenever they are needed.
- As teams begin to make visits, they should avoid the mistake of leaving completed forms in their leader's kit. The administrators cannot do their work unless the forms are turned in on time.
- Team leaders and members should look for ways to improve their kits and share their improvements with other teams. (If teams will send their suggestions to the address on page 83, the author can share new ideas with an even wider audience.)

5. Now discuss your plans for using a filing system. If you already have an administrative system in place, you may use this exercise to show and explain the components of your working system. (If an administrator is available, ask him or her to help you present and explain this system.) If, on the other hand, you are just starting out in LRE, you may use this exercise to brainstorm ideas for materials, equipment, and personnel with the class. (Welcome the expertise that individual class members may have as a result of their jobs or other experience.) Key questions for those just starting out include:

- Who will be responsible for securing what resources?
- When will these resources be secured in order to have them available for the start of visitation in two weeks?
- Who would be good candidates for your ministry's administrators (assuming these are not already in place)?
- Who will recruit them and by when?

Whether you are just starting out or already in operation, make a sketch on newsprint or on a chalkboard of ideas as they are presented. For example, draw a flow chart of the movement of forms through each of the following steps: 1) during the visit, 2) at the report session, 3) to the administrator, 4) into a time-sensitive file, 5) back to a team for a follow-up visit, 6) into a general file, etc. Above all, be realistic. If you have a computer, use it to your advantage. If you only have a file cabinet at this time, that is also fine. Just decide what is best for your situation and start with that. In everything you do and say, be sure to emphasize the importance of administration for a ministry that depends on building long-term relationships.

6. Ask the members of the class to reflect on their learnings during this session by answering the following questions.
   - What is the most helpful thing I learned during this session? What was the most interesting topic or exercise?
   - How will what I have learned help me grow spiritually closer to Christ?
   - What would I like the class to study more closely?

7. Preparing for Next Session:
   - **Participants:** Read Part One, Chapter 8, on the role of the Holy Spirit in the ministry of visitation. Pay special attention to the two concepts at the heart of this chapter: *divine appointments* and the *power of presence.*
   - Meet with a prayer partner during the coming week and discuss the following questions. Keep a diary of your responses, and be prepared to share your thoughts at the next session.
     — Did the Holy Spirit place someone in my path today or this week with whom I could build a relationship, meet a need, or share my experience of faith? Did I do what I could? If not, why not?
     — Have I sensed a burden for someone today or this week? If so, what have I done about this?
     — In what ways can I grow more sensitive to the nudgings and promptings of the Holy Spirit in the course of everyday life?
   - **Trainers:** Next week is the final training session before actual visitation begins. As a result, you need to be prepared next week to give ministry teams their working assignments, including a personalized map designating each ministry area, a standard schedule for regular visitation (see sample on page 44), and any final adjustments of team composition or personnel that have been needed or requested.

8. Close this session by inviting team members to read aloud together the following prayer:
   Lord Jesus, thank you for the ministry of administration. Strengthen those who are gifted for this ministry in our congregation. We recognize the importance of this aspect of evangelism. May we never see it simply as paper work, for it is also an intentional and disciplined way of caring. Strengthen us too as we move closer each week to becoming like those original seventy disciples that you sent out. As we prepare to go out in your name, we know that none of us will ever be the same again. We love you and trust you to work through us for the sake of your kingdom. Amen.

SESSION 6
Following the Holy Spirit

The best planning and training available cannot replace the power and presence of the Holy Spirit in the ministry of evangelism. Fortunately, planning and following the Spirit are not mutually exclusive. Indeed, the best approach of all is to plan *and* to follow the Spirit. In this way teams will be prepared to conduct their ministries in an orderly and disciplined manner, yet remain open to the ever-changing possibilities that real ministry always entails.

In preparation for this final session participants should have read Part One, Chapter 8 on the role of the Holy Spirit in the ministry of visitation. Teams will discuss the role of the Holy Spirit in evangelism and will leave the building briefly to explore their new ministry areas. The final event of training is the Covenant of Evangelism Service. This should be a high and holy moment, characterized by enthusiasm and optimism. The pastor must be included in the planning for this service and, ideally, he or she will lead the service. Families, friends, and even the whole congregation can also be invited to participate in the service as a way of broadening ownership for the commissioning of the new LRE teams. (If you would like to have a personal, written message of encouragement from the author of this volume to share during the Covenant of Evangelism Service, contact me at least one month in advance of your date at the address on page 83.) This session will last longer than all others. You should be able to complete all activities in two hours. If your class would like to have refreshments after the covenant service, that will take some additional time.

Purposes for Session 6

- To reflect together on the implications of Jesus' promise to send his disciples forth in the power of the Holy Spirit
- To encourage participants to share their own experiences of divine appointments
- To give teams an opportunity to enter their actual ministry areas for the first time
- To share in a covenant service for evangelism ministry

> ## ❖ Outline for Session 6 ❖
>
> 1. Getting Focused *(10 minutes)*
>
> 2. Opening Prayer *(5 minutes)*
>
> 3. The Power of the Spirit *(20 minutes)*
>
> 4. Exploring New Ministry Areas *(20 minutes)*
>
> 5. Covenant of Evangelism Service *(45 minutes)*

Materials Needed

- Extra Bibles for participants who did not bring their own for this session
- Maps of new ministry areas mounted on cardboard
- A small notebook for each team of three to use to take notes as they travel to their new ministry area
- An order of worship for the Covenant of Evangelism Service (developed in consultation with the pastor or other designated staff member of the congregation)
- Elements for sharing the sacrament of Holy Communion (bread, cup, etc.)
- Attractively printed cards giving the date for the first experience of actual visitation (to be given to participants as a tangible reminder of their commissioning as lay ministers in LRE)

1. Help teams focus on the theme for this final session by calling the class to order and inviting participants to consider the role of the Holy Spirit in the account of Hinton Brown. First, remind the class of the highlights of Hinton's story (page 73). Then, invite the class to consider the implications of this layman's story for their own experience of following the Spirit. Ask for volunteers to respond to the following questions.

   - How does this account make me feel personally? Why?
   - How can we as Christians be more sensitive to the possibility of divine appointments in our daily lives?
   - What should we do to demonstrate wisdom in the way we talk about divine appointments with family, friends, and other members of the congregation, some of whom may be skeptical of this kind of experience?

2. Lead (or ask one of your team leaders to lead) the class in a time of opening prayer. Continue to emphasize the centrality of prayer in this ministry, and encourage participants to continue sharing their prayer concerns and using their notebooks in the weeks ahead as they become engaged in regular visitation. Close this time of prayer by inviting participants to pray aloud together the following prayer.

   Come, Holy Spirit, fill our hearts with your love and grace. Grant us your power that we may go into the field of need to minister according to your guidance. We are seeking to be faithful in reaching out to those who are inactive as well as to those who have never heard the good news of Jesus Christ. Open our hearts to your leading that we may not be hindered by what others think. Remove from us any negative stereotypes concerning you and your work in the world. Draw us closer to each other and closer to you in all things. In Jesus' name we pray. Amen.

3. Continue to work with the class as a whole and invite participants to share their own experiences of following the Holy Spirit. Instruct them to use the notes they made in their diaries during the past week and invite volunteers to respond to the following questions.

   - What was the most surprising thing the Holy Spirit revealed to me in this past week?
   - What were some ways I responded to the leading of the Holy Spirit in this past week?

- What happened as a result of my response?
- Were there times in the past week that I felt led to do something and then backed away from that feeling? Why?

Close this exercise by reading aloud Acts 1:8,

> *"But you will receive power when the Holy Spirit has come upon you; and you will be my witnesses in Jerusalem, in all Judea and Samaria, and to the ends of the earth."*

After the reading, invite the class to discuss the questions that follow. (Note: Acts 1:8 is a *promise*, not a question or a hypothetical statement. Luke was confident that the Spirit would come and, when it did, Jesus' followers would discover power to be his witnesses in ways they might heretofore have considered impossible.)

Questions:
- What is the nature and purpose of the power that is given to Christians?
- What relevance does this promise hold for us in the church today?
- How can we live this out in the practical round of our daily lives?

4. Now instruct the teams to go out for the first time into their new ministry areas. The purpose here is to help participants get excited about their new areas, and to make some initial notes on the physical, social, and other characteristics that they discover. Distribute maps of the new ministry areas to the teams. Direct each team to go into its area, to drive through slowly, and to observe all that they can. They might pay special attention to the following.

- What kind of homes are here? How many are well kept?
- How old are the homes? Are any for sale?
- Are there children in this area? What evidence indicates their presence or absence?
- What is the general feel we get from driving through this area?

Give the teams fifteen minutes to complete their initial exploration, and instruct them to keep notes on their discoveries to share with other teams when they return.

5. As the final event of training, hold a special Covenant of Evangelism Service. The importance of this service cannot be overemphasized. It will be a time of commissioning for team members. They now go forth into the field of need as ministers of evangelism for their local church. It will stir the hearts of family members and others in the congregation who support the congregation's ministry of evangelism. It will also set the tone for this new ministry in the minds of many who may be exposed to LRE for the first time. Therefore, though the form of the service will vary greatly depending on the creativity of each congregation, certain elements should without doubt be included:

- Ask the pastor to work with LRE leaders in designing this service of celebration.
- Celebrate Holy Communion around the theme of being commissioned for Christ.
- Sing enthusiastic hymns of faith.
- Include at least one testimony from a new team member.
- Arrange for special music on the theme of evangelism (solo or choir).

- Ask the pastor or other leader to prepare a powerful sermon on the great commission (Matthew 28:18-20) or another passage that expresses the biblical basis for LRE.
- Be sure that one of the LRE leaders gives a clear and concise description of the vision and purpose of LRE at some point during the service.
- At the close of the service, invite all participants to come to the front of the sanctuary to be commissioned by the pastor and others standing with or behind them.
- Give each commissioned team member one of the cards with the date for the first experience of actual visitation.
- Invite the whole congregation to pray with the teams as all anticipate how the Lord will work through them on the first night of visitation.
- Above all, give thanks and celebrate.

For Further Reading

The following titles are available from Discipleship Resources, P. O. Box 189, Nashville, TN 37202, (615) 340-7284.

Faith-Sharing: Dynamic Christian Witnessing by Invitation, by George E. Morris and H. Eddie Fox.

Vision 2000: Planning for Ministry into the Next Century, by Joe A. Harding and Ralph W. Mohney.

Caring Evangelism: A Visitation Program for Congregations, Leader Guide and Participant Workbook, by Suzanne G. Braden and Shirley F. Clement.

Tried & True: 11 Principles of Church Growth from Frazer Memorial United Methodist Church, by John Ed Mathison.

Every Member in Ministry: Involving Laity and Inactives, by John Ed Mathison.

Incorporating New Members: Bonds of Believing, Belonging, and Becoming, by W. James Cowell

Extending Your Congregation's Welcome: Internal Climate and Intentional Outreach, by W. James Cowell.

Appendices

APPENDIX A
Special Instructions for United Methodist Men

As described in Chapter 1, the ministry of LRE first began to spread in The United Methodist Church as a result of the support and experience of United Methodist Men. The relationship between LRE and United Methodist Men has continued to be strong and supportive through the years, leading in 1993 to the presentation of LRE as an official program of United Methodist Men and the General Board of Discipleship at the International Congress of United Methodist Men at Purdue University. With this background in mind, therefore, we would be remiss if we did not describe in some detail how local chapters of United Methodist Men can become the primary sponsor for LRE in their congregations.

What does a local chapter of United Methodist Men need to know in order to sponsor LRE? Naturally the contents of this book — reading material and training sessions — are foundational. In addition, two other components need to be described: 1) possible roles for United Methodist Men officers and other leaders in support of LRE, and 2) extended support opportunities for the local church through other United Methodist Men groups and through the author. Let's look at each of these in turn.

President of United Methodist Men

The President of United Methodist Men is an active member of the local church and gives overall leadership to the United Methodist Men's fellowship. He presides at meetings of the fellowship and handles many of the necessary administrative functions. He is also a regular member of the congregation's Council on Ministries and, therefore, has direct input into the ministry plans adopted by the congregation. As a result, the president of United Methodist Men is in a good position to provide leadership for the consideration of LRE both as a special ministry of United Methodist Men and as a general ministry of the congregation.

The president's leadership might include several steps. First, he should work closely with the pastor of the congregation, keeping him or her informed of plans for LRE (see Chapter 4 for detailed instructions). The president could also establish a task force of United Methodist Men leaders to study LRE as presented in this book, to begin their own practical experience with visitation, and to arrange for the first study of LRE in the congregation. Eventually, study sessions for the whole congregation could be offered under the sponsorship of United Methodist Men. The president of United Methodist Men could be both a participant in the pilot study and a trainer in the subsequent study sessions.

Vice President

The vice president in many United Methodist Men's fellowships is in charge of programs for regular and special meetings. As such, he is in a good position to invite guest speakers and presenters from other United Methodist Men groups who have already started LRE.

This can be a key motivation for other men in the fellowship, helping them catch the vision of genuine outreach evangelism.

The vice president might also serve as the primary recruiter for LRE. Working closely with the secretary of United Methodist Men, he could contact all the men in the fellowship and invite them to come to an introductory meeting to consider the ministry of LRE. Then, on the basis of personal contacts, he could help set up the class roster for the pilot study. As a recruiter, he would also need to be thoroughly familiar with this book as a whole, and especially with Chapter 4. Naturally, the vice president would also be one of the first participants in the pilot training group and would continue to work closely with the president as the ministry expands to other members of the congregation.

Secretary

The secretary of United Methodist Men should have a current comprehensive listing of all men in the congregation who are involved in the fellowship. Using this list as a resource, he can work with the vice president in the process of inviting men to general exploratory sessions and in recruiting specific men for the special training sessions. As such, the secretary should also be thoroughly familiar with the contents of this volume and should be invited to participate in the pilot study.

In addition, the secretary might also be asked to compose a letter of invitation to the local chapter of United Methodist Women, inviting them to recruit a number of their members to be part of the pilot study. (Remember, LRE teams work best with members of both genders.) This letter should be upbeat and clearly definitive of this new ministry. This may be the first time United Methodist Men and Women have participated in a joint study and training session for the benefit of the entire congregation. (A powerful thought indeed!)

Prior to sending this letter, the president, vice president, and secretary of United Methodist Men should meet with the leaders of United Methodist Women to discuss the ministry of Lifestyle Relational Evangelism. This meeting should be informal and in a comfortable setting. It should also cover certain basic issues:

- The vision of men and women working together to launch a new ministry
- The model for leadership that is envisioned (Depending on local needs and resources, training responsibilities might either be shared among men and women, or left primarily in the hands of United Methodist Men.)

In any case, this new cooperative relationship should only strengthen the ministry of visitation and help the entire outreach efforts of the congregation. A cooperative effort with United Methodist Women and the Council on Ministries will go a long way to change the posture of the congregation to one of genuine outreach evangelism.

LRE Director

Each local United Methodist Men's fellowship will also need to choose someone to serve as the director of LRE in the congregation. This person will be responsible for the basic, ongoing operations of the ministry. He could serve as primary trainer for the pilot study group or designate someone to serve as the primary trainer for this group. At the very least, he will be part of the pilot group, a definite leader of LRE ministry in the congregation, and a regular participant in subsequent weekly training and visitation.

Choosing the right person for this position is critically important. Much prayer should go into the selection process. This person should be chosen by the president, vice president, and secretary in consensus. It would be wise, though not necessary, to include the pastor in this selection process, as he or she is the chairperson of the nominations committee of the congregation. As a guideline, the man chosen for this position should exhibit the following personal and spiritual characteristics.

- A readily apparent personal relationship with Jesus Christ as Savior and Lord
- Experience sharing his own testimony in a loving and effective way with others inside and outside the congregation
- A heartfelt passion for evangelism in the local church, a strong conviction that the church should be involved in outreach in an ongoing way
- A reputation as a legitimizer in the local church, someone to whom others listen, a respected leader in the congregation
- A strong, positive, supportive relationship with the senior pastor of the congregation
- Active involvement in Sunday school and worship services
- Deep belief in the power of prayer and an active prayer life that is known to persons in the congregation

This person will not be easy to find. He will need to be willing to commit himself to work for at least two years on the establishment of LRE in the congregation. Moreover, he will need to surround himself with other members in United Methodist Men and in the congregation who have similar characteristics in their Christian witnesses.

Opportunities for Extended Training

As a result of the historic involvement of United Methodist Men with the ministry of LRE, local chapters of United Methodist Men have opportunities for extended training. The basis of this extended training is a plan developed in Douglasville, Georgia, by Proactive Evangelism Ministries, Inc., of which Jim Hollis is Executive Director, in conjunction with the central office of United Methodist Men in Nashville, Tennessee. The plan is to create a group of LRE consultants to serve as trainers and initiators of LRE in conferences all across North America.

The first group of consultants to receive extended training will have come together (by the time you read this) at the International Congress of United Methodist Men at Purdue, July 1993. Since this volume is being published prior to the Congress (for use during the Congress) it is not now possible to determine the exact number of consultants who will have been trained or their locations around the country. Nevertheless, the goal of the LRE home office and the central office of United Methodist Men is to have three United Methodist Men consultants in every conference of The United Methodist Church who can serve as trainers and initiators of LRE in their areas, under the guidance of the Home Office of Proactive Evangelism Ministries, Inc.

What can you do to find out about training possibilities in your area? Since the network of consultants and trainers is being coordinated by the author of this volume, you can simply call or write to the address on the following page:

James W. (Jim) Hollis Jr.
Proactive Evangelism Ministries, Inc.
6800 Green Oak Drive
Douglasville, GA 30135-4553
1-404-949-9674 (Office and Fax)
CompuServe Mail: ID # 71477, 112

In turn, the LRE home office will work with you to determine the best way to arrange for extended training in your congregation. This might include calling on either conference United Methodist Men consultants (if available), other congregations in your area who have already begun their ministries of LRE, or arranging for training through the staff of Proactive Evangelism Ministries itself. In any event, every effort will be made to have extended training available, designed for your needs and situation.

Conclusion

Every local chapter of United Methodist Men has the potential to bring dynamic, positive change to its congregation through sponsoring and leading Lifestyle Relational Evangelism. The ideas given above are really only a starting point for each chapter's creativity. My prayer is that your United Methodist Men chapter and many others will pray about participating in this ministry, then develop your own new ways to effectively sponsor LRE. I am confident that you will see significant results as you follow the Lord in spiritual growth and outreach. Press on in the Spirit and move out beyond the walls with our Lord, who is able to lead us all.

Appendix B
Basic LRE Training: Mini-Weekend Model

One of the options for scheduling LRE training is the Mini-Weekend Model training event. As described previously on page 82, this model calls for training in three areas: motivation, education, and experience. The training is conducted, moreover, in coordination with an instructor and a team of trained laypersons from outside the host congregation. Below is a brief description of the plans and goals for each session of a typical two-day event. (Longer training events focusing on the same components can also be scheduled.)

Friday Evening: Motivation

Fellowship Meal
- Introduce the instructor and training team members.
- Distribute nametags to all participants.
- Team members get to know members of the congregation as they sit and eat together.
- People ask questions about LRE in informal conversations.

Service of Praise and Celebration (immediately following the meal)
- Focus on the theme "Evangelism Possibilities with Christ" and on breaking down the negative stereotypes that people carry about evangelism.
- Plan special music.
- Lay trainers share their experiences of LRE.
- Someone on the team delivers a highly motivational sermon.
- People are invited to come forward at the close of the service to affirm new commitments and for a time of prayer at the altar.

Small Group Sharing
- Members are placed in groups of five to eight according to a number written on their nametags.
- Each group is led by a member of the training team who shares more about what the ministry of LRE has meant in his or her life.
- Groups discuss informally what it means for laypersons to become directly involved in local church evangelism — their feelings, hopes, fears, questions, and visions.
- Groups bring their discussion to a close with a circle of prayer before participants depart for the evening.
- Host families take training team members home where sharing typically continues, sometimes far into the night.

SATURDAY MORNING: Education

Breakfast
- Everyone meets at the church for an early breakfast.
- Sharing and fellowship from the previous evening continue, usually at a more profound level as interest and excitement build.

Educational Component
- The instructor and training team lead participants in three hours of practical training on the theory and methods of LRE.
- Training is comprehensive in scope and is presented in a variety of ways, such as lecture, music, drama, video, testimonies, and role play.

SATURDAY AFTERNOON: Experience

Lunch
- Morning instruction comes to a close with the serving of lunch.
- Lunch conversation builds with excitement as participants anticipate going out for actual visits.

The Experiential Component
- Training team members (laity and clergy) lead local church participants (laity and clergy) in actually going out into the community to make calls in the homes of unchurched persons.
- Participants now experience first hand what the motivational and educational components were all about.
- Participants' apprehensions typically melt away as they experience the power of reaching out in a positive way to people in their community who might never walk into a local church on their own.
- Participants begin to see themselves inside the vision of LRE and to believe that God will use them to build relationships and meet needs for Christ.

Closing Service of Sharing and Celebration
- After the visits are complete, everyone returns to the church building for a time of sharing and celebration.
- Report forms are filled out by each team and turned in to the administrators (who will also be trained).
- Team members write personalized cards to the individuals and families they visited, expressing appreciation for the opportunity to meet and get to know them as new friends.
- Each team also shares a summary of its experience in the field with the whole group.
- The joys of one team are shared by all, as are the frustrations of another.
- A bond of togetherness in mission forms — even in this short time — that will carry the congregation forward in the weeks to come, as it continues with further training and visitation.

My staff, laity, other clergy, and I lead numerous training events across North America. Many churches choose to expand the Mini-Weekend Model into a Full Weekend Model, utilizing Saturday evening and Sunday morning worship and Sunday school to further enhance this new ministry in the congregation. Call or write the Home Office for details.

Appendix C
Supporting Ministries

Every congregation needs a variety of supporting ministries that serve as "doorways" through which unchurched persons and inactive members can find their way into active relationship with Christ and the church. Most congregations have a few of these doorways or entry ports simply by default — for example, Sunday school, United Methodist Men, United Methodist Women, and others that are common — but every congregation also needs new entry ports for new people. New doorways can often be created with relative ease, offering access for new persons who seek a way into the circle of friendship and fellowship. Let's look at some of these.

Sports Ministries

One of the most effective entry ports for new people is a solid sports ministry in the congregation. I suppose nearly every congregation in the southern United States either has a softball program or wants one, but softball is not the only sport that can serve in this way.

Other congregations offer basketball, volleyball, golf tournaments, tennis matches, croquet teams, racquetball tournaments, soccer, flag football, and other organized sports that provide a variety of entry ports for persons of all ages, backgrounds, and ability levels. The ultimate purpose of a sports ministry is not simply to play games, however; it is to have fun, share fellowship, and build relationships.

Great care must be taken in the development of a sports ministry, or it can become narrow and self-defeating. At worst, a sports ministry can develop into an exclusive group of egotistical amateur athletes who simply wear the church's name on their team jerseys. Such teams are not really for ministry at all, and they can cause many hard feelings in a congregation. On the other hand, if properly organized, a sports team can be one of the finest forms of ministry in the congregation.

Effective programs require a director of sports ministries for the congregation. This person should be prayerfully and carefully chosen by the committee on nominations. He or she must be a person who has a deep desire to see as many people as possible become involved in sports through the congregation. This person will not be satisfied with anything less than widespread involvement of people both inside and outside the congregation at all skill and ability levels. Usually, wisdom dictates that this person not be one of the key players on any team. Rather, he or she serves as the overseer and greatest encourager of all teams.

In order to truly support the ministry of evangelistic outreach, the entire sports ministry should be organized to encourage the development of relationships among many different persons both inside and outside the membership of the congregation. For example, if the church softball team is part of a league that plays on Saturday nights at a large local park, then the members of your congregation will have opportunities to meet a variety of people who come out to cheer for the teams. Not only will you meet and get to know the members of other congregations in your area, but you will also find that unchurched people and inactive members of your own congregation come out for such an event. In this way, Saturday night may become "church family night" in your area, and many people will have an opportunity to see the church in a positive light.

The key to all of this, however, is your congregation's capacity to *include* people of every skill and interest level in your sports ministry. Skill and interest levels come in four basic varieties:

1. Moderate to strong athletic ability
2. Little athletic ability but a desire to play
3. Undeveloped yet potential ability
4. No athletic ability but a desire to support the sports ministry itself

Skill Level 1 is an obvious starting place for building and designing a sports ministry in many congregations. The danger, however, is that a congregation will focus its entire sports program on skilled athletes and will do little or nothing to include the other skill levels. When this happens, the possibilities for ministry are greatly diminished.

Highly skilled athletes usually have some major goals in mind when they join a team — typically, to win, to win, and to win. There is nothing wrong with winning. Everyone loves to be a winner. Competition adds drama to the game. In fact, if we were not playing to win, then why would we keep score? An all-consuming passion to win, however, can be harmful to the potential development of relationships. It can lead to supercharged competition that excludes persons who don't measure up physically to the best athletes on the team. This atmosphere can turn more people away than any losing record ever did. An overemphasis on winning can also teach young people in their formative years that winning is everything. Persons who feel they absolutely have to be winners often make a poor witness for the church by arguing with umpires, shouting at the other team, or being visibly angry over losing. At this point, fans no longer see a sports ministry; they witness simple egomania. For all of these reasons, we must not limit our teams to just the best athletes.

The other three skill levels mentioned above are in many ways more important for a sports *ministry*. For one thing, they contain the largest number of potential players, coaches, helpers, and spectators. Each of these skill levels will, however, require creative encouragement and development. For example, a congregation might create a team called "The Over-the-Hill Gang" made up of persons who want to play softball (or another game) primarily for fun. This team could literally fill up the stands and become a real conversation topic in the local community. Athletic ability would not be a primary requirement for this team. In fact, those who have athletic ability might be steered away from this team altogether, unless they are prepared to adopt a truly serving role as trainer, coach, or mentor. This type of team provides yet another entry port into the church via the sports ministry.

An effective sports ministry should also keep in mind that youth have enormous undeveloped athletic ability. With the proper encouragement, young people can develop a wonderful team. Such teams often attract youth who would otherwise never darken the door of a church building. Moreover, the families of these unchurched young people will be right there to cheer them on as they play. This can be a wonderful facet of the church's sports ministry. Word of this will spread through the schools and community as a positive witness for the local church. A church that invests wisely in youth is a church that attracts families.

As a congregation's sports ministry develops, the person who serves as the director will need help. He or she should thoughtfully choose persons to serve on a committee that will lead the sports ministry. The committee should be composed of all the coaches or managers of the various teams and other persons in the congregation who enjoy being spectators at these events. This committee will keep in mind that the primary goals of this ministry are fellowship and relationship building and will do everything possible to see that the organization fosters these primary goals. This will insure that the largest number of persons possible will be included in the wonderful entry port of sports ministry.

Video Ministry

Since everyone is not interested in sports, congregations need other entry ports as well. Another effective doorway into the congregation can be created around something nearly everyone enjoys — videos.

Enormous numbers of video cameras and equipment have been purchased by families and individuals in recent years. No doubt there are people in your congregation and community who own such equipment. Most of this equipment is quite expensive and infrequently used except for special family occasions; yet people are usually delighted to have an opportunity to make use of their equipment, especially for the cause of ministry. Just think of the events in your congregation that might be taped by an active group of video buffs and shown later as part of a special program. Here are some ideas:

- Sports events sponsored by the congregation might be taped and shown as part of the entertainment for Wednesday night suppers. People love to see themselves on tape and to laugh at the ups and downs of a sporting event.
- Worship services of the congregation might be taped and shared with shut-ins using a portable VCR unit hooked to their television sets. This is greatly appreciated.
- Youth retreats or other special events outside the local church setting can be taped in order to share memories with the folks back home, as well as with those who attended the events.
- Musical performances by the choirs can be taped and copies distributed to relatives, friends, shut-ins, and others.
- Teaching series by various church leaders might be taped and used by home Bible study groups, sharing groups, fellowship groups, and individuals. This would be one way to expand and extend the teaching ministry of your pastor.

A list such as this can be expanded in many directions. Use your imagination. Some congregations even tape weddings and other special events for families and use the income for special projects. Most persons with video equipment are excited to be invited to share in this type of ministry. Their involvement gives them a place to serve, and it opens the life of the congregation to new people in a variety of ways. That is what an entry port is all about.

35mm Photography

Video is only one way to create a visual image that can be meaningful in ministry. Nearly every family or individual you meet — both inside and outside the congregation — owns a set of photographs that record personal and family events. Why not keep albums of photo memories for the church family as well? After all, many people of all ages immensely enjoy the hobby of 35mm photography. What is a hobby for these people can also become a form of ministry, as they take pictures or slides that record the family history of your congregation.

As visitation teams go into their ministry areas each week, they could bring some of these pictures with them to share. They could even create an album of photos portraying various facets of the congregation's life and ministry. What better way to give the people visited a taste of what it is like to be part of your church family? Visual images of the church at worship, work, and play reveal more than words alone could every convey. They give an intimate glimpse into the lives of those who make up your congregation, and they invite others to come and see.

Bulletin boards offer another significant opportunity to use 35mm photography. Placed strategically throughout the church building, and attractively arranged with photographs of various activities and events, bulletin boards convey a sense of the vitality that is part of the ongoing life of your congregation. They proclaim that something exciting is happening around here. It is amazing how much can be communicated by a well designed display.

Health and Fitness

Many congregations have successfully developed a ministry of fitness or aerobics. Some have done this in conjunction with the construction of family life centers or other such facilities, though these are not required. All that is needed is a good VCR, a television, and a large room (preferably carpeted) where a group can work out. A fitness ministry can be conducted in conjunction with a weight loss program for members of the congregation and community, or it can be organized just for the purpose of exercise and fun.

A good fitness program in the church offers an alternative to the atmosphere that prevails in many commercial spas and clubs. Though health clubs are ostensibly for personal improvement, their focus on physical beauty and strength sometimes backfires with ironic results. Such facilities often have an impersonal air. Though crowded with people, they can be very lonely places. Persons who do not have the body of a model, moreover, may be intimidated by those who manage to stay in top physical condition.

By contrast, a fitness program in the church can be focused on the total health of those who take part — mind, body, spirit, and life in community. Exercise classes can be organized for many different age groups and held at different times during the week. A good variety of times and intensities will appeal to the largest number of persons. Such classes can become the focus of friendship and fellowship for those who attend. They also lead naturally to other kinds of involvement — for example, a sharing group, Sunday school class, or a Bible study. When people share the grit and sweat of working out together over a period of time, they often develop a common bond of openness and trust. This is the basis for a relationship and an open doorway into the fellowship of the church.

Bicycling

Another port of entry into the fellowship and ministry of the local church can be reached by bicycle. Cycling is one of the most popular sports in the United States today; millions of people own bikes. More and more individuals and families are choosing cycling as a sport to enjoy with friends. The majority of these bikes and bikers, however, never leave their own street or neighborhood.

Why not start a cycling club in your congregation? Unlike some other sports, cycling is open to practically anyone. People old and young, large and small, can enjoy a bike ride and take it at their own pace. With the latest developments in cycling, even families with small children can participate. A wide variety of equipment is available: infant carriers that easily attach to adult bicycles, bike trailers for infants and children, and even tandem bikes for riding together. The cost of such equipment is not great. All of these options make it more feasible than ever for young couples with children to get in on the sport of cycling. As a result, cycling can build bridges between generations in a wonderful way. Moreover, there is no real competition in cycling for fun and fitness. Rather, a true sense of fellowship and comradeship develops, as people begin to log miles together.

As a bicycling club develops, the members can begin to plan day trips together. Such trips serve both to build relationships in the groups and to get in touch with new areas in the surrounding community. For example, a club might plan regular rides bimonthly or even weekly, leaving from the church parking lot. The group could start out with short rides and build up to more advanced tours. There might be a ride from the church building to a restaurant or park along the route where the group could stop and enjoy a meal together before making the return ride. Clubs can also adopt funny or interesting names (for example, "U.M.P.S." for "United Methodist Pedalers' Society") and they can make T-shirts for members to wear.

A well organized and widely traveled bike club will make an impact on the surrounding community. People in the community will want to know who that group of bikers is. Some will want to take part in an activity that is so much fun. A bike club is a great vehicle for helping others find their way into the life and ministry of the church.

Conclusion

Ports of entry are simply activities that enable persons who are currently outside the fellowship of the local church to find meaningful and fun ways of entering. As such, they are also ministries in their own right, ministries that build relationships, meet needs, and ultimately lead to the grace and love of Jesus Christ. As people find their way into an activity, they also find new friendships. As they work at enhancing these friendships, they also discover in new ways what life in the church could mean for them. There are persons in your community who will be attracted to the church through a sports ministry, a fitness program, or a cycling club, who would otherwise never consider coming to the church building.

Those who are involved in support ministries as members of the congregation have a wonderful opportunity to discover the meaning of ministry in the context of friendship. They will want to be sensitive to the needs of their new unchurched friends as the latter explore what this involvement in church is all about. As relationships grow through the activities of the support ministry, moreover, the interest of unchurched persons in the meaning of church and faith will often grow as well. The challenge for members of the congregation is both to care for the relationship and to offer ways of deepening the spiritual meaning of the relationship through entry into other activities such as Sunday school, sharing groups, and worship services.

Support ministries exist ultimately for the purpose of helping those who are unchurched to find their way into a personal relationship with Christ and the church. As unchurched people come to share in these groups, they will find that church people are not like the stereotype that exists in our culture. Church people are real human beings who struggle and play, care and rejoice, as they seek to follow the Spirit of Christ. All of this provides a much needed vantage point for hearing anew the claims of Christ and considering his place at the center of life.

APPENDIX D
Role Playing Resources

Variations of individual and family situations are virtually endless. The following sketches illustrate a few of the kinds of situations visiting teams will encounter as they go out into the field of need in their ministry areas. Use these ideas as starting points for your own imaginations. Develop your own different scenarios to use in portraying families and individuals who might be visited. Keep your role playing ideas realistic, or they will not help teams deepen the skills needed for actual visitation.

Possible Household Situations

1. You are a family — husband and wife with three children: boy (16), girl (12), and boy (3) who was adopted last year. You had to move from a large city as the result of a job transfer required of one of the spouses. The other spouse has specific skills and is currently looking for a job. Your uncle is also with you; he came to look for a job as well.

2. You are a single father (31), divorced, with two children — boy (11) and girl (6). Each child is from a different marriage. Your mother who is elderly (78) has come to live with you in your apartment since her husband (your dad) passed away two months ago. You have lived in this neighborhood for the last three years but have not been involved in church since 1968.

3. You are three young men who room together. You were involved in the same fraternity at the university where you graduated. You are all in your mid-twenties. One of you is a pharmacist. One works in financing. One is a computer consultant. All of you are dating at this time, but none of you are seriously involved with anyone. You are very busy on weekends with sports and other leisure activities. The computer consultant, whose dad is a minister, has a strong background in the church, and is feeling that he should get involved again in a congregation nearby. The financier has a serious drinking problem, but the other two roommates don't know how to help. As it happens, he calls while the visiting team is in the house to tell his friends he has just been arrested for D.U.I. and is in jail.

4. You are a young couple in your early twenties. You have a brand new baby and are full of hope and very friendly. You are interested in coming to church, but there is one thing that you are afraid will be a problem if you reveal it — you are not married. You have some definite stereotypes about how people in a church will treat you if they know of your situation. Individually, you are afraid about where your future may lead.

Possible Occupations

banker	auto mechanic	stewardess	teacher
master chef	garbage collector	doctor	dentist
lawyer	landscape worker	dental hygienist	store clerk
principal	politician	police officer	baker
waitress	FBI agent	social worker	psychologist
trucker	country singer	real estate agent	executive

Possible Needs That Could Be Met

teen pregnancy	trouble with police	D.U.I. arrest
death of spouse	serious illness	loneliness
AIDS	marriage separation	job loss
credit card debt	unexpected lawsuit	auto wreck
cancer	abusive spouse	child abuse
baby with Down's Syndrome	adultery	cult influence
hurtful church memory	parent with Alzheimer's disease	gunshot wound
broken bones	upcoming surgery	

Possible Personality Traits of Those Being Visited

religious fanatic	hostile to strangers	overbearing salesman
tremendous pain	extreme loneliness	open anger
agnostic	ignorant of Christianity	universalist
open and friendly	shy but receptive	nervous
preoccupied with TV	illiterate	

Possible Settings for Casual Acquaintance Visits

physician's office	sports event for kids	restaurant lobby
car repair center	tire store lobby	bus
airplane	supermarket line	house party
picnic	convenience store checkout	fast food line
carpools	club meetings	hairstyling salon
houseboat	fishing tournament	bicycle tour
soccer game	family style restaurant	block party
I.R.S. office	attorney's office	waiting line